PEAK DISTRICT
>> TRAIL RUNNING

22 OFF-ROAD ROUTES FOR
TRAIL & FELL RUNNERS

VERTEBRATE PUBLISHING

Design and production by Vertebrate Publishing, Sheffield
www.**v-publishing**.co.uk

PEAK DISTRICT
» TRAIL RUNNING

22 OFF-ROAD ROUTES FOR
TRAIL & FELL RUNNERS

Nikalas Cook & **Jon Barton**

PEAK DISTRICT
>> TRAIL RUNNING
22 OFF-ROAD ROUTES FOR
TRAIL & FELL RUNNERS

VG Copyright © 2014 Nikalas Cook, Jon Barton & Vertebrate Graphics Ltd.

VP First published in 2014 by Vertebrate Publishing.

Nikalas Cook and Jon Barton have asserted their rights to be identified as the authors of this work.

ISBN 978-1-910240-14-4

Front cover: Jenny Stafford-Curtis and Becky Lounds running along Curbar Edge (route 7).
Back cover: Ian Winterburn on Doctor's Gate (route 21).
Photography by Keith Sharples unless otherwise credited.

All maps reproduced by permission of Ordnancy Survey on behalf of The Controller of Her Majesty's Stationery Office. © Crown Copyright. 100025218.

Design and production by Jane Beagley.
www.v-graphics.co.uk
Printed in Slovenia by Latitude Press Ltd.

MIX
Paper from
responsible sources
FSC® C110418

>> CONTENTS

≫ INTRODUCTION

There is no special requirement to trail-run in the Peak; no mystery, no fitness or special temperament is needed, just a will to enjoy fresh air and great scenery, and a be-prepared-for-a-bit-of-exhilaration attitude.

That said, some of the routes in this book are hard work. Some are boggy, long and gruelling, others are hard to navigate. But not all of them. Many of the routes are pleasant and relatively flat, covering short, manageable distances and even starting and finishing from a cafe, or, better still, a pub serving Sunday lunch.

All corners of the Peak District are covered here; some famous trails are run along, while some less frequented and windswept patches of moorland are traversed. Some are our favourite 'secret' runs, others popular with many. Some of the runs, like the Ladybower, Carsington and Monsal Trail/Bakewell jaunts, are great for those new to running, or those who like running in safe and friendly parts of the Peak. The harder, more challenging routes, such as the outings on to the Peak's one true mountain, Kinder Scout, and its surrounding uplands, can be serious undertakings – especially in the winter months. They make a good choice if you're an experienced runner looking for a challenge.

So, go shopping if you must, get some new trail shoes, a few gel bars and maybe a running pack, but most importantly get out there and start putting one trainer in front of the other. Don't worry about how fast or slow you go, feel free to walk up the hills, and stop every now and again and listen to the birdsong and enjoy the view.

Happy running!

Nikalas Cook & Jon Barton

ACKNOWLEDGEMENTS

Nikalas: Thanks to my most consistent and reliable running companion, Otso the Lapp-hund, and also the two-legged company of Paul, Rory and my long suffering wife Lissa.

Jon: Thanks to contributors, photographers, testers and running pals: Thomas Barton, Gráinne Coakley, Keith Sharples, Steve Franklin, Claire-Jane Carter, Ben Winston, Paul Bennett.

ABOUT THE ROUTES

The routes range in difficulty from relatively flat trail runs that should take less than an hour to bog-trotting upland epics that have the potential to take up to five hours. We have listed the runs within the book in order of increasing distance. If you're unsure about your ability, aren't familiar with the area or come from a road running background, start with some of the easier routes to gauge your level.

MAPS

All the routes are carefully described and plotted on Ordnance Survey 1:25,000 mapping, but we strongly recommend that you carry the relevant full map (if for no other reason than that they weigh less!) and a compass. **Explorer OL1 The Peak District – Dark Peak Area**, and **Explorer OL24 The Peak District – White Peak Area** cover all the runs in this guide and are essential even if you are familiar with the area – you may need to cut short a run or take an alternative route. And of course, a map is no use without the navigational skills to use it.

DESCRIPTIONS, DISTANCES & ASCENT

While every effort has been made to ensure accuracy within the maps and descriptions in this guide, we are unable to guarantee that every single detail is correct. Please exercise caution if a direction appears at odds with the route on the ground. If in doubt, a comparison between the directions, map and a bit of common sense should ensure you're on the right track.

Distances are in kilometres and height gain is in metres. Both were measured using GPS devices on the runs, but we cannot promise that they are 100% accurate, so please treat stated distances as a guideline only. Our estimated times are a combination of optimism, generosity, challenge and fiction; just allow plenty of time and try to run an even pace.

TERRAIN

We have attempted to describe the terrain on each route, but of course it can be dramatically influenced by the weather. Streams become swollen, rocks slippery and moorland boggy. If you venture on to Kinder, Bleaklow or Black Hill after a wet period, don't expect to be setting any PBs. That said a number of the routes can be described as all weather, for example the Monsal Trail/Bakewell run.

RECOMMENDED EQUIPMENT

Recommended kit varies depending on the time of year and the difficulty and nature of the route. While many runners like the freedom of a 'fast and light' approach, longer and more remote runs are best undertaken with a little more kit.

» **Bag:** there are plenty of lightweight rucksacks and bumbags on the market. Find one that's comfy and doesn't move around on rough ground.
» **Waterproofs/windproofs:** jacket and trousers. We'd strongly recommend fully waterproof with taped seams, this is the Peak District.
» **Hat and gloves:** keep your extremities warm and the rest will follow. It's no fun fumbling with shoelaces with frozen fingers.
» **Map and compass:** and know how to use them! The relevant maps are listed on page VIII.
» **Whistle:** Six short blasts in quick succession means 'help!'
» **Space blanket and small first aid kit:** weigh nothing, takes up hardly any room and could save your life.
» **Food and water:** enough for your expected duration of the run and some emergency rations.
» **Headtorch:** if you're heading out late, a headtorch should be high on your list of essentials.

FOOTWEAR

We'd recommend at least 'trail' shoes for all these routes, with fell shoes being desirable on the harder routes. Trail shoes offer more grip and greater stability than road shoes, while the deep lugs on the sole of fell shoes will come in handy on boggy or wet ground.

CLOTHING

Dress appropriately for the season. Shorts and a vest work well on hot summer days, but thermals, windproofs and gloves are better on winter runs. Please note that exposure on higher ground is a very real risk for the tired, lost or slowing runner – better to carry a small bag with full waterproofs and gloves/hat, than be flapping around on the top of Kinder trying to get a signal and call out mountain rescue.

FUEL & HYDRATION

Hot days can be deadly for the trail runner. We don't recommend drinking from any streams in the Peak, so carry sufficient water (either in bottles or a hydration pack) for your run. Likewise, a banana or two and an 'emergency' gel can come in handy, especially on long days out.

SAFETY

Ideally, run in pairs, tell someone where you are going and carry a phone – but note that finding good reception is difficult in many parts of the Peak. Should you find yourself out of reception, be grateful to be temporarily free of the phone's tyranny.

MOUNTAIN RESCUE

In case of an accident or similar requiring mountain rescue assistance, dial 999 and ask for **POLICE – MOUNTAIN RESCUE**. Be prepared to give a 6-figure grid reference of your position in the case of a moorland location.

MOUNTAIN RESCUE BY SMS TEXT

Another option in the UK is contacting the emergency services by SMS text – useful if you have a low battery or intermittent signal. You need to register first – text 'register' to 999 and then follow the instructions in the reply. **www.emergencysms.org.uk**

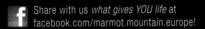

THE COUNTRYSIDE CODE

BE SAFE – PLAN AHEAD

Even when going out locally, it's best to get the latest information about where and when you can go; for example, your rights to go on to some areas of open land may be restricted while work is carried out, for safety reasons or during breeding seasons. Follow advice and local signs, and be prepared for the unexpected.

» Refer to up-to-date maps or guidebooks.
» You're responsible for your own safety and for others in your care, so be prepared for changes in weather and other events.
» There are many organisations offering specific advice on equipment and safety, or contact visitor information centres and libraries for a list of outdoor recreation groups.
» Check weather forecasts before you leave, and don't be afraid to turn back.
» Part of the appeal of the countryside is that you can get away from it all. You may not see anyone for hours and there are many places without clear mobile phone signals, so let someone else know where you're going and when you expect to return.

LEAVE GATES AND PROPERTY AS YOU FIND THEM

Please respect the working life of the countryside, as our actions can affect people's livelihoods, our heritage, and the safety and welfare of animals and ourselves.

» A farmer will normally leave a gate closed to keep livestock in, but may sometimes leave it open so they can reach food and water. Leave gates as you find them or follow instructions on signs; if walking in a group, make sure the last person knows how to leave the gates.
» In fields where crops are growing, follow the paths wherever possible.
» Use gates and stiles wherever possible – climbing over walls, hedges and fences can damage them and increase the risk of farm animals escaping.
» Our heritage belongs to all of us – be careful not to disturb ruins and historic sites.
» Leave machinery and livestock alone – don't interfere with animals even if you think they're in distress. Try to alert the farmer instead.

PROTECT PLANTS AND ANIMALS, AND TAKE YOUR LITTER HOME

We have a responsibility to protect our countryside now and for future generations, so make sure you don't harm animals, birds, plants or trees.

» Litter and leftover food doesn't just spoil the beauty of the countryside, it can be dangerous to wildlife and farm animals and can spread disease – so take your litter home with you. Dropping litter and dumping rubbish are criminal offences.

» Discover the beauty of the natural environment and take special care not to damage, destroy or remove features such as rocks, plants and trees. They provide homes and food for wildlife, and add to everybody's enjoyment of the countryside.

» Wild animals and farm animals can behave unpredictably if you get too close, especially if they're with their young – so give them plenty of space.

» Fires can be as devastating to wildlife and habitats as they are to people and property – so be careful not to drop a match or smouldering cigarette at any time of the year. Sometimes, controlled fires are used to manage vegetation, particularly on heaths and moors between October and early April, so please check that a fire is not supervised before calling 999.

KEEP DOGS UNDER CLOSE CONTROL

The countryside is a great place to exercise dogs, but it is owners' duty to make sure their dog is not a danger or nuisance to farm animals, wildlife or other people.

» By law, you must control your dog so that it does not disturb or scare farm animals or wildlife. You must keep your dog on a short lead on most areas of open country and common land between 1 March and 31 July, and at all times near farm animals.

» You do not have to put your dog on a lead on public paths as long as it is under close control. But as a general rule, keep your dog on a lead if you cannot rely on its obedience. By law, farmers are entitled to destroy a dog that injures or worries their animals.

» If a farm animal chases you and your dog, it is safer to let your dog off the lead – don't risk getting hurt by trying to protect it.

» Take particular care that your dog doesn't scare sheep and lambs or wander where it might disturb birds that nest on the ground and other wildlife – eggs and young will soon die without protection from their parents.

» Everyone knows how unpleasant dog mess is and it can cause infections – so always clean up after your dog and get rid of the mess responsibly. Also make sure your dog is wormed regularly.

CONSIDER OTHER PEOPLE

Showing consideration and respect for other people makes the countryside a pleasant environment for everyone – at home, at work and at leisure.

» Busy traffic on small country roads can be unpleasant and dangerous to local people, visitors and wildlife – so slow down and, where possible, leave your vehicle at home, consider sharing lifts and use alternatives such as public transport or cycling. For public transport information, phone Traveline on 0871 200 2233.

» Respect the needs of local people – for example, don't block gateways, driveways or other entry points with your vehicle.

» By law, cyclists must give way to walkers and horse riders on bridleways.

» Keep out of the way when farm animals are being gathered or moved and follow directions from the farmer.

» Support the rural economy – for example, buy your supplies from local shops.

ACCELERATE

Sheffield & the Peak's only specialist Trail
Running Store. www.accelerateuk.com
@accelerateuk #RunningRedefined

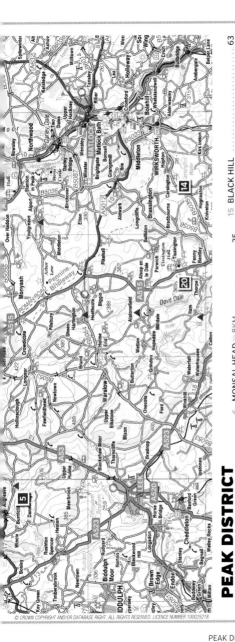

PEAK DISTRICT TRAIL RUNNING

AREA MAP

THE
TRAILS

Some of these runs you'll enjoy, some you won't.
Some you'll do with friends on a lovely summer
evening, some you'll grind out, enveloped in mist
and alone, thinking you're lost on a mountainside.
Some of the runs are perhaps too short for your long
wiry legs, some a little long as you regret not taking
that extra energy bar. Rest assured though we
have done our best to share with you our favourite
trails in the Peak District. Our runs are in order
of increasing length, but short doesn't necessarily
mean easy ... so read the description, study the map,
lace up your shoes and get out there!

01 ≫ LANGSETT

5km

INTRODUCTION

A short run tracing a loop around Langsett Reservoir. Starting with well-manicured trails and then crossing the bridge over the Little Don river, it heads up and out across Hingcliff Common to the old ruins of North America. From here it drops into the woods of Midhope before crossing the dam and following good trails back to the car park.

THE ROUTE

There is a well surfaced path all the way around Langsett Reservoir, and for the most part this satisfying trail run makes use of it, with one crucial deviation: a short excursion on to the 'wild' moorland of the Dark Peak. So in a little over five kilometres the terrain goes from woodland trails and shoreline paths to rocky moorland bridleways and peaty plodding. There's even a short bit of tarmac, just in case you were regretting buying this book and are longing for the carefree days of pounding around suburbia. Navigation is easy – just keep the water on your left and the moorland on your right.

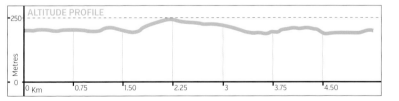

ALTITUDE PROFILE

250 — Metres — 0

0 Km   0.75   1.50   2.25   3   3.75   4.50

≫ LANGSETT

DISTANCE 5KM ≫ *ASCENT* 126M ≫ *MAX ALTITUDE* 250M ≫ *TYPICAL TIME* 0:45 HRS ≫ *TERRAIN* WELL SURFACED WOODLAND, SHORELINE AND MOORLAND TRAILS ≫ *NAVIGATION* GOOD TRAILS AND A BIT OF WAYMARKING MAKE FOR EASY NAVIGATION ≫ *START/FINISH* LANGSETT BARN CAR PARK ≫ *GRID REF* SE 210004 ≫ *SATNAV* S36 4GY ≫ *OS MAP* EXPLORER OL1 THE PEAK DISTRICT – DARK PEAK AREA ≫ *REFRESHMENTS* BANK VIEW CAFE, LANGSETT TEL: 01226 762 337

DIRECTIONS ≫ LANGSETT

S From the car park, drop down the well-surfaced trail towards the shore of the reservoir. **Turn right** on to a good trail and follow the water's edge for about a kilometre. **Keep left** at the fork and then **turn left**, steeply downhill, to a bridge over the stream. **Take the left hand gate** and, passing a map sign, proceed uphill.

2 Keep on this trail as it swings back right and climbs steeply and rockily (i.e. don't go on to the Yorkshire Water concessionary footpath along the water's edge). Keep heading uphill, less steeply now, and after about 500m **turn left** on an obvious path by a green sign. The trail is good and level, soon dropping down towards a ruin known as North America. **Keep straight ahead** on an improving surface, soon dropping down to cross a stream. Pass through a gate 80m after the crossing, and, as the good track swings back right, **go straight ahead** on to a concessionary footpath along the shoreline.

3 Follow this footpath. TAKE CARE after 500m – follow the path where it swings uphill (beware a less defined track does continue straight ahead at this point). Meet a surfaced track after going through a small gate. (If you meet a road first, just hop over the wall and turn left!)

4 **Turn left** and follow the track to where it meets the road. **Turn left** and follow the road downhill. Cross the dam and immediately afterwards take a footpath on the **left**. Follow this for 50m, then **turn right** on to another path to return to the car park (or do another, faster lap!).

GRÁINNE COAKLEY AND SON, MOORLAND RUNNING >> *PHOTO* JON BARTON

INTRODUCTION

The route starts by following the Monsal Trail, then turns off to climb over Cracknowl via a good path before dropping into Bakewell. A token bit of riverside running and a quick climb lead to Bakewell Station and back on the Monsal Trail to the start.

THE ROUTE

The Monsal trail is the Autostrada of trails, a weaving throng of horses, prams, wheelchairs, ramblers with poles, ramblers without poles, children, dogs on long leads, dogs on short leads, children on long leads, children on short leads and bikes. Oh the bikes, everything from whirring electric affairs to the hire fleet, the odd normal person on a normal bike and a few grown men stretching Lycra way beyond its design parameters.

We happily run through this, because we love the wide open spaces trail runs like these take us through. Of course, if you venture on to the trail outside the sunny Sunday afternoon rush hours, it is usually quiet and empty. And in winter this well-surfaced route gives a pleasant short run no matter what the conditions.

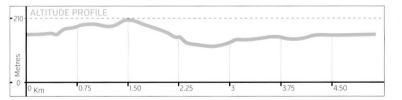

» THE MONSAL TRAIL

DISTANCE 5.3KM » *ASCENT* 90M » *MAX ALTITUDE* 210M » *TYPICAL TIME* 0:45 HRS » *TERRAIN* GOOD, WELL SURFACED TRAILS » *NAVIGATION* EASY TRAILS » *START/FINISH* HASSOP STATION CAFE AND BOOKSHOP » *GRID REF* SK 217706 » *SATNAV* DE45 1NW » *OS MAP* EXPLORER OL24 THE PEAK DISTRICT – WHITE PEAK AREA » *REFRESHMENTS* HASSOP STATION CAFE TEL: 01629 815 668

DIRECTIONS » THE MONSAL TRAIL

S   Drop on to the Monsal trail from the back of the car park, and **turn right**. Go under the bridge and after approximately 300m **turn left** through a gate, off the trail and on to a well-signed bridleway. Follow this narrow path gently uphill through a number of gates and over the top of the hill before eventually dropping on to a wider track, into the trees and past tumbledown buildings towards a tarmac road.

2   **Turn left** and follow the road for a short way, then take the grassy footpath across the field on the **right**, towards the river. Where it meets two gates, go through the **right hand gate** and continue along the river to the bridge. Leave the path and, not crossing the bridge, **turn left** and head uphill towards the car park/industrial estate on Station Road. Climb **straight ahead** (not right towards the car park) and at the top follow the road around the bend and then **turn right** into the small Monsal Trail car park.

3   Re-join the Monsal Trail by taking the narrow path to the **left** of the converted station building. **Turn left** on the trail and race 2km back to the start.

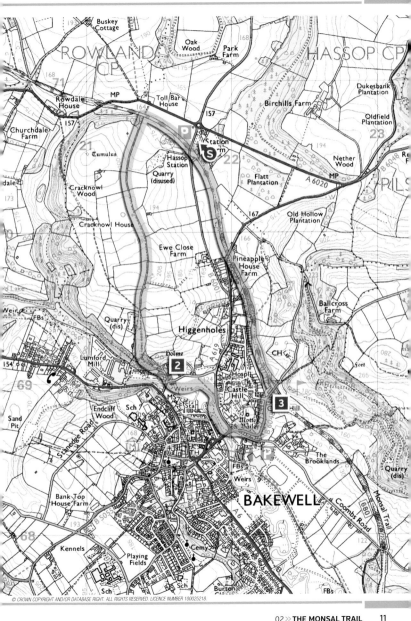

CLAIRE-JANE CARTER ON THE CLIMB FROM CUTTHROAT BRIDGE >> *PHOTO* JON BARTON

INTRODUCTION

This short route gives a glimpse into the world of the long-distance fell runner: where our route loops back homewards, the ridgeline of Derwent Edge continues, tantalising and runnable, into the far distance, dissolving into open rugged moorland.

THE ROUTE

From the start the route climbs beautifully, initially up grippy gritstone blocks, then across open moorland, and then steeply and briefly up on to Derwent Edge. A tricky path now loops across Derwent Moors, leading down and back round to the start. With excellent views, good trails and lovely surroundings, this is as satisfying a 5k run as you might ever do.

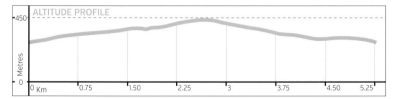

ALTITUDE PROFILE

>> **DERWENT**

DISTANCE 5.4KM >> **ASCENT** 155M >> **MAX ALTITUDE** 450M >> **TYPICAL TIME** 0:40–1:00 HRS >> **TERRAIN** MOORLAND PATHS >> **NAVIGATION** GENERALLY EASY, BUT THERE ARE JUNCTIONS AND THE ROUTE TAKES IN SOME HIGH GROUND >> **START/FINISH** SMALL CAR PARK CUTTHROAT BRIDGE, OR LARGE LAY-BY UP THE HILL IF CAR PARK FULL >> **GRID REF** SK 213873 >> **SATNAV** S33 0AX (NEAREST) >> **OS MAP** EXPLORER OL1 THE PEAK DISTRICT – DARK PEAK AREA >> **REFRESHMENTS** LADYBOWER INN TEL: 01433 651 241

DIRECTIONS ≫ DERWENT

S From the small car park at Cutthroat Bridge (park in the larger lay-by up the road if this is full), cross the road and head up the rocky, blocky track that begins just at the downhill end of the bridge. Head uphill with the stream on your right on to the moor. Stick with the track as it swings left and then right, heading up on to the moor proper and watch out for the odd hurtling mountain biker! The gradient, while uphill, is just right to set a good pace, and before you know it (well, after a lung-bursting 10 minutes) the crossroads at Whinstone Lee is reached. Pause not!

2 **Turn right**, steeply uphill. Stick to the vague ridge and grim in, the path is all very hard work, but unlike any other hill climb it really does ease off just over the next brow. You can do it. After the initial 250m, the gradient eases and, with great views in all directions, continue to climb steadily. 1km after Whinstone Lee a crossroads of paths is reached at a small dip in the ridge. **Turn right** here, following the path downhill alongside the beautifully manicured grouse butts.

3 A long descent crosses open moorland with the track gradually becoming more defined. Ford a stream and continue descending through a gate and under the power lines. After another gate, take the stile on the **right**, as the main track heads left towards Moscar House (a couple of hundred metres away). Follow this path, over more stiles, until it drops down to and crosses the stream. Step up and **turn left**. If all has gone well Cutthroat Bridge should be just in front of you.

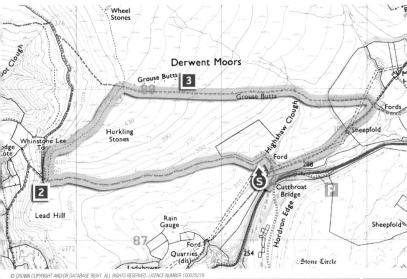

PAUL REEVE AND DAUGHTER SOPHIE BEGINNING THE CLIMB OF CARL WALK

INTRODUCTION

The classic evening run or winter head clearer for the local Sheffield crowd. Beautiful undulating terrain makes up the first half, crossing rocky escarpments and prehistoric forts, while the second leg follows a 'fast' pacey track back up to the start. The basic run can be made shorter or longer (or *much* longer), depending on how much of the valley is traversed.

THE ROUTE

Heading south from the car park the route keeps to the Burbage skyline, first climbing over and dropping off one knoll, then climbing up and over the second (Higgar Tor) before dropping again to cross a third knoll – the ancient fort of Carl Wark – and twisting down through grassy moorland to the road. Turning left, the run crosses Toad's Mouth bridge and joins the Burbage Green Drive for a pleasant and never too steep climb through the heart of the Burbage Valley. Passing under the gritstone crags of Burbage South and North, and high above the Burbage Brook, the wide and easy trail loops up the east side of the valley and back to the start.

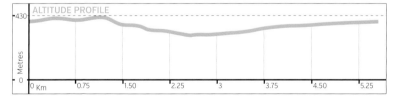

>> BURBAGE VALLEY

DISTANCE 5.5KM >> *ASCENT* 160M >> *MAX ALTITUDE* 430M >> *TYPICAL TIME* <1 HR FOR THE INITIATED >> *TERRAIN* MIXED, WITH SOME BOGGY GROUND AND ROCKY CLAMBERING >> *NAVIGATION* MOSTLY EASY ALTHOUGH NOT ALL ON OBVIOUS PATHS >> *START/FINISH* LARGE LAY-BY OR CAR PARK AT BURBAGE BRIDGE >> *GRID REF* SK 260830 >> *SATNAV* S11 7TS [NEAREST] >> *OS MAP* EXPLORER OL1 THE PEAK DISTRICT – DARK PEAK AREA >> *REFRESHMENTS* NORFOLK ARMS, RINGINGLOW TEL: 0114 230 2197

DIRECTIONS >> BURBAGE VALLEY

S From the large car park just west of Burbage Bridge, exit via the small gate and head south keeping to the **right-hand track** on the top of the knoll – don't be tempted to follow the good track that looks like it circumnavigates the first knoll, as it stops in a few metres at a lovely welcoming bench. Follow the broad (muddy in winter) boulder- and bedrock-strewn route over the knoll, soon dropping down on to a more distinct path, heading for the next hill. Climb up this on steps and then continue over the top, **keeping left**. At the escarpments **keep straight ahead** and scramble down through the rocks heading for the main descending path (finding the correct route to scramble down is half the fun).

2 Continue descending to the col. (A shorter version of the route turns left here to descend to the stream and then climb a short distance up to the green drive.) We continue **straight ahead**, climbing up and over the top of Carl Wark hill fort. As we drop off the far side, paths go off in all directions – keep heading more or less **straight ahead** on vague and always boggy tracks. Keep the next rocky edge/escarpment just to your left and curve around it on a now obvious path which drops down to the road.

3 **Turn left** and jog up the road, crossing the bridge and heading uphill before **turning left** into the small car park. Head through this, via two gates, on to the Green Drive, a wide and well-surfaced track. Steady, good pacey running now, sometimes a little rocky, leads back up to Burbage Bridge. Go through the gate and left along the road* back to the car park. (*Alternatively, avoid the road by taking the narrow path alongside the wall and scrambling down and across two slippery stream crossings.)

ALTERNATIVE ROUTE

A more challenging route returns along the top of the Burbage edge, instead of the Green Drive, but we think the Green Drive is such a lovely track, full of climbers, walkers, prams, dogs, sheep and all manner of humanity it would be a shame not to join in.

To take this alternative route, **turn right** on grassy tracks not long after joining the Green Drive, and then **trend left** through the maze of sheep tracks, heading for the top of the edge. Once up, follow the obvious rocky track along Burbage South edge. As you begin to descend, keep to the main track and ignore turnings to climb up on to the top of Burbage North edge. Once again, follow the obvious track along the edge, this time, to the road.

INTRODUCTION

A good circuit in one of the more secluded corners of the Peak District. Navigation along well-signed paths is easy enough, while the terrain is constantly changing, dropping through layers of woodland alongside the River Dane and traversing pasture farmland before heading back over exposed moorland.

THE ROUTE

Initially following the course of the pleasant River Dane on sometimes muddy trails, the run heads downstream to Danebridge and the meeting of Black Brook with the Dane. From here, good woodland running leads along the valley. Always interesting, it's more thought-provoking than fast: sometimes muddy and sometimes rooty, with the odd low branch to duck. Eventually the route emerges into meadowland, covered in all sorts of goats and sheep. Climbing up and around the top of the hill gives far-reaching views out across the surrounding countryside, before a good, wide trail drops off the moors and down through the splendidly-named Forest Wood, past the rock formations at Lud's Church and back to the Dane and then the start.

The route can easily be extended by heading south along the stunning – and obvious – ridgeline of the Staffordshire Roaches.

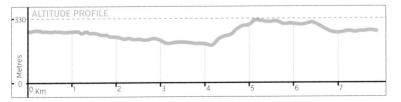

ALTITUDE PROFILE

» **GRADBACH**

DISTANCE 8KM » *ASCENT* 260M » *MAX ALTITUDE* 330M » *TYPICAL TIME* 0:50–1:15 HRS » *TERRAIN* WOODLAND AND MOORLAND TRAILS, MORE PUDDLES THAN BOGS WHEN WET! » *NAVIGATION* MOSTLY STRAIGHTFORWARD ON GOOD WAYMARKED TRAILS » *START/FINISH* DERBYSHIRE WILDLIFE TRUST CAR PARK, GRADBACH » *GRID REF* SJ 997662 » *SATNAV* SK17 0SU » *OS MAP* EXPLORER OL24 THE PEAK DISTRICT – WHITE PEAK AREA » *REFRESHMENTS* FLASH BAR STORES TEL: 01298 22763

DIRECTIONS >> GRADBACH

S Leaving the car park, head down the road taking the **right fork** down to the Youth Hostel. Head into the front yard of the hostel, then **straight on** down the signed public footpath. Follow this through gates and stiles, up and down a little, to cross a small footbridge. At the sign, continue **straight ahead** towards *Swythamley/Lud's Church*, but after a few metres, **turn right** at another fingerpost signed *Danebridge* (you can go right at the first fingerpost also signed *Danebridge*, just be careful not to get too close to the river as you'll then have to scramble up the bank to the main path).

    Good woodland running continues, always interesting and more thought-provoking than fast, before the route heads into meadowland and then dives back into the wooded river valley to drop down to Danebridge.

2 Just before the trail joins the road at Danebridge, and where it is running close to the water, a gate and steep stone steps appear on the **left**. Take this, all very hard work for a couple of minutes but soon easing off to a merely steep and good trail leading up through the trees.

3 Follow the trail out of the trees and up across the field. Go through the stile in the wall and **keep heading right** and uphill. Join a better lane which leads past a farm, under the Hanging Stone, and towards another house, Paddock Farm/Cottage. Head almost to their front gate, where the path is then well signed to the **left**. Follow this, and then at the junction take the path **left** signed *Lud's Church/Gradbach*.

4 Climb up a little way on to the moor and keep on the good path, often waterlogged! Head over the hill and down the other side for a good long stretch through the woods, ignoring turnings as you go. Eventually, meet the fingerpost just by the footbridge and retrace your steps to the Youth Hostel and then back up the road to the car park.

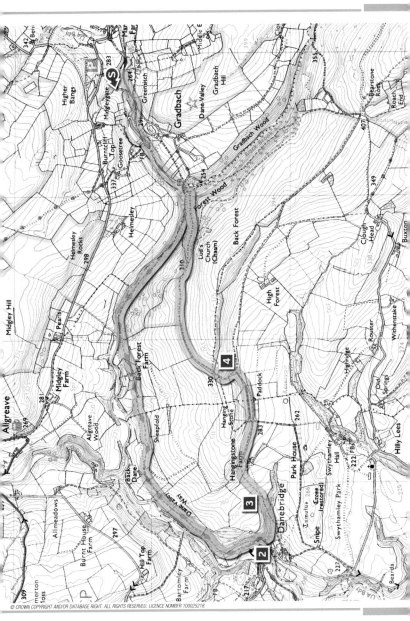

06 ⟩⟩ MONSAL HEAD   8km

INTRODUCTION

An interesting short route that mixes up some fairly technical steep climbing and descending with flat, well surfaced and very runnable trails. Running through the two tunnels on the Monsal Trail is great fun and the route as a whole would be a good head to head race between an all-out fell runner and a roadie.

THE ROUTE

Resist the lures of the pub, cafe and ice-cream van and head down on to the Monsal Trail. The initial steep, rocky and stepped path rewards accomplished and nimble descenders but you're quickly on the flat, running along the trail and crossing the spectacular viaduct. If it's the weekend you'll be weaving round walkers, cyclists and horse riders, but plough on – running through the Cressbrook and Litton tunnels makes the crowds worthwhile. Run on a quiet day and they're eerily still and quiet. After the tunnels, leave the trail and climb steeply before enjoying fast running on grassy trails. Apart from the regular gates, it's then super quick running on undulating semi-metalled roads and tracks before the path narrows and steepens for the descent back to the Monsal Trail. You're now back on the viaduct and, if you're a mountain goat, looking forward to the steep climb to the finish. If you're not so fond of climbing, think of the pint, cake or 99 flake that's waiting at the top.

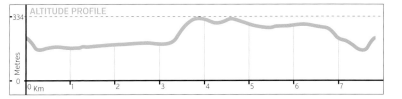

ALTITUDE PROFILE
334
Metres
0
0 Km   1   2   3   4   5   6   7

⟩⟩ MONSAL HEAD

DISTANCE 8KM ⟩⟩ *ASCENT* 315M ⟩⟩ *MAX ALTITUDE* 334M ⟩⟩ *TYPICAL TIME* 1 HR ⟩⟩ *TERRAIN* MOSTLY EASY TRAILS, BUT SOME ROCKY CLIMBS AND DESCENTS THAT CAN BE SLIPPERY IN THE WET ⟩⟩ *NAVIGATION* VERY EASY TO FOLLOW TRAILS ⟩⟩ *START/FINISH* MONSAL HEAD CAR PARK ⟩⟩ *GRID REF* SK 185715 ⟩⟩ *SATNAV* DE45 1NL ⟩⟩ *OS MAP* EXPLORER OL24 THE PEAK DISTRICT – WHITE PEAK AREA ⟩⟩ *REFRESHMENTS* HOBB'S CAFE, MONSAL HEAD TEL: 01629 640 346; MONSAL HEAD HOTEL TEL: 01629 640 250

DIRECTIONS » MONSAL HEAD

S   **Turn left** on the road out of the car park and then **immediately left again** to take you past the front of the pub and cafe. Look for the fingerpost pointing the way down to the viaduct and Monsal Trail.

2   **Cross the viaduct** and follow the trail through the Cressbrook and Litton tunnels. Older OS maps do not show the tunnels as they've only recently opened but it's fairly obvious where they go. You can get maps of the whole Monsal Trail, showing all of the tunnels.

3   About 500m after emerging from the Litton Tunnel, you'll come to a footbridge over the trail and a footpath off to your left. **Take this footpath** and climb steeply, sticking to the obviously worn track. As the ground levels off, continue to follow the trail across the fields until you come to a gate and a semi-metalled road. Go through the gate and **turn left** on to the road. Stay on this track for approximately 4km, going through the village of Brushfield, a fair few gates and following signs to Monsal Dale.

4   Stay on the trail as it descends steeply, narrows, becomes rockier and then eventually spits you back out on to the Monsal Trail. **Turn right** on to the Monsal Trail, cross back over the viaduct and retrace your steps to climb back up to Monsal Head.

JENNY STAFFORD-CURTIS AND BECKY LOUNDS ON CURBAR EDGE

9km

INTRODUCTION

The headline run here heads out from the car park and follows the good cliff-top track along the tops of Froggatt and Curbar Edges before heading up on to the moors and the summit of White Edge. The edge is followed for several pleasant kilometres before the run drops through the woods and pastures under White Edge Moor, heading for the welcoming sight of the Grouse Inn.

THE ROUTE

There are two runs here, the first is a gentle trail run, starting from and, crucially, finishing at an excellent pub. It's a mostly flat stretch on a well surfaced trail, making its way through delightful woods as the view opens up across the wide and scenic Derwent Valley. Those after such an 'adventure' may turn back at the first hill (or, if you're slightly more intrepid, at the Curbar Gap car park), retrace their strides and call it a day. Otherwise, the run really kicks in from Curbar Gap, heading across the moor and up on to the moorland escarpment of White Edge. The trail now narrows, becoming rockier and more technical, and the running, while never hard, requires stamina, especially if you want to maintain a good pace and make it round in a respectable sub-hour time.

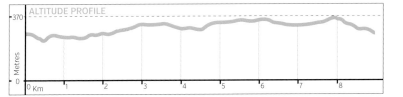

>> **FROGGATT, CURBAR & WHITE EDGE**

DISTANCE 9KM >> *ASCENT* 250M >> *MAX ALTITUDE* 370M >> *TYPICAL TIME* 1–1:30 HRS >> *TERRAIN* MOORLAND TRAILS, WELL DRAINED >> *NAVIGATION* STRAIGHTFORWARD ON GOOD TRAILS >> *START/FINISH* LAY-BY JUST BELOW THE GROUSE INN, OR LARGER NATIONAL TRUST CAR PARK A LITTLE FURTHER DOWN THE ROAD >> *GRID REF* SK 257778 >> *SATNAV* S11 7TZ (NEAREST) >> *OS MAP* EXPLORER OL24 THE PEAK DISTRICT – WHITE PEAK AREA >> *REFRESHMENTS* THE GROUSE INN TEL: 01433 630 423

DIRECTIONS » FROGGATT, CURBAR & WHITE EDGE

S From the lay-by, head down the road and into the National Trust car park. Take the small path at the far (bottom) end of the car park, cross the stream and clamber up the steep bank to the road. Cross the road and head downhill a short way to a gate on the **left** – head through this on to an excellent trail. Follow the fast and well-surfaced trail through the woods, through a gate and out on to the open ground above Froggatt Edge, where the good running continues.

2 At the short, steep hill you have a choice: head directly up for a rocky but short lived scramble, or keep left for an easier time. The good trail resumes at the top with excellent views. A few more minutes of good striding and all too soon you've done the first 4km and are through the gate at the end of the edge. **Keep left** into the Curbar Gap car park. If the weather is 'awful' or you are just in the mood for a trail run, turn around and head home.

3 Our run continues out of the car park. At the exit from the car park, turn **immediately left** through a gated stile next to a farm gate and continue along the wide grassy path, taking the **right fork**. Follow this, crossing a muddy stream via a bridge. Run hard up a steep bank and, at the top, **turn left** at the T-junction on to White Edge.

4 Follow the obvious track along the edge. It's more or less flat with some fast running and plenty of twists and rocks to bound across. Very satisfying. Eventually you meet a wall – **turn left**, downhill, and **then left** again into the trees. Go through the gate and, mud permitting, a lovely sprint down across the field leads to the road. **Turn left**, jog downhill to the lay-by (and then **right** back into the car park).

INTRODUCTION

On any given Sunday all the car parks and lay-bys within five miles of Ladybower will be jammed with cyclists, walkers, climbers and runners, all sat on their tailgates, pulling on a pair of shoes and getting on with the fun part of the week. This is for good reason: the Upper Derwent valley is all mountains and lakes. Some very tough fell runs traverse this region, but there is also an abundance of perfect low level, all-weather trail running, none finer in our opinion than this circum-navigation of Ladybower Reservoir.

THE ROUTE

From Fairholmes car park, head out towards the dam on tarmac. Turning south along the eastern shore of the reservoir, the road soon turns to track, which undulates down towards the main A57. Cross the reservoir on the much-photographed bridge, then follow the trail back along the western shore to the car park. Even in the depths of winter the well-surfaced trail is smooth and mud-free, and normal trainers or trail shoes are fine. Nowhere is the route exposed and while there is a surprising amount of height gain it is all easily won on good tracks with fantastic (and distracting) scenery.

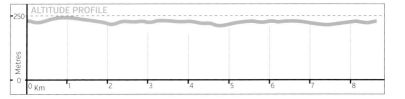

ALTITUDE PROFILE

≫ **LADYBOWER TRAIL RUN**

DISTANCE 9KM ≫ *ASCENT* 280M ≫ *MAX ALTITUDE* 250M ≫ *TYPICAL TIME* 0:45–1 HRS
≫ *TERRAIN* GOOD, WIDE TRACKS THROUGH WOODLAND ≫ *NAVIGATION* EASY, ON GOOD TRAILS
≫ *START/FINISH* FAIRHOLMES CAR PARK ≫ *GRID REF* SK 171893 ≫ *SATNAV* S33 0AQ (NEAREST)
≫ *OS MAP* EXPLORER OL1 THE PEAK DISTRICT – DARK PEAK AREA ≫ *REFRESHMENTS* REFRESHMENTS
KIOSK, FAIRHOLMES TEL: 01433 650 953

DIRECTIONS >> LADYBOWER TRAIL RUN

S From the car park, head out north past the cafe and follow the path on to the road downhill, curving rightwards under the dam wall. Keep to the road, now heading uphill. At the top of the rise ignore turnings and **keep straight ahead**, now running southwards on the eastern side of the reservoir. Continue to ignore turnings and the tarmac turns to good hardpack track, undulating over streams and through woodland, finally passing through a wide gate and joining tarmac at the main road bridge on the A57.

2 **Turn right** across the bridge, and then, once across the reservoir, **turn right again** through a gate on to a path. Follow this path north up the western shore of the reservoir. The first hill is the only significant climb on this route and ground is easily won through the trees. All too soon the car park is reached. Ice creams for the sub-50 minuters!

FINISHING SPRINT ALONGSIDE ERRWOOD RESERVOIR

09 ≫ SHINING TOR

9.2km

INTRODUCTION

A run of two halves – one up, one down – on clear and easy-to-follow paths that'll give less experienced runners, who might not be too confident with a map and compass, the chance to experience high moorland terrain.

THE ROUTE

Heading out of the car park, you're soon steadily gaining height on a root-ridden trail. Crossing the minor road known as The Street, you pick up a trail that runs parallel to it and continues grinding uphill. The surface is generally good but there are boggy patches. You can always detour around them on the road, but you're a trail runner aren't you? Leaving the security of roadside trail, you turn on to the moors, climbing steadily to Cats Tor. By now you have stone flags under your feet, a controversial tool of moorland management, but they do make climbing and route finding easy. A brief descent gives you a chance to steel your legs before the final grind up to Shining Tor. On a clear day the view to the Cat and Fiddle and the distinctive Shutlingsloe hill is stunning. Now, let your legs go and enjoy the descent. Starting off on oddly springy hardpack, after a final brief uphill kick, it's a fun, fast, furious and open downhill all the way back to the reservoir.

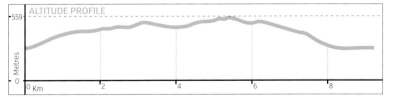

ALTITUDE PROFILE

≫ SHINING TOR

DISTANCE 9.2KM ≫ **ASCENT** 296M ≫ **MAX ALTITUDE** 559M ≫ **TYPICAL TIME** 0:50–1:50 HRS ≫ **TERRAIN** MIXED, INCLUDING SOME HIGH MOORLAND ≫ **NAVIGATION** EASY CLEAR TRAILS ≫ **START/FINISH** ERRWOOD RESERVOIR NORTHERLY CAR PARK ≫ **GRID REF** SK 014756 ≫ **SATNAV** BUXTON [NEAREST] ≫ **OS MAP** EXPLORER OL24 THE PEAK DISTRICT – WHITE PEAK AREA ≫ **REFRESHMENTS** WHALEY BRIDGE

DIRECTIONS » SHINING TOR

S   **Head north** out of the top end of the car park, keeping the road to your right. As the road bears left, cross it, **turn left** and then follow the path that runs parallel to the road. After just under 2km, you'll see a fingerpost pointing right to Windgather Rocks, ignore it. Carry on for a short while, then **turn left** across the road, go through the gate and take the obvious uphill path.

2   Follow this path that becomes flagstones and stay on it all the way to the summit of Shining Tor. At the summit (the trig point is hidden on the right hand side of the wall), **turn left** and follow the path downhill.

3   After a brief rise, you'll come to a fingerpost pointing **left** to Errwood Reservoir. Follow this path all the way down and through a car park to the road that runs along the shore of the reservoir.

4   **Turn left** and follow the road over an inlet channel. Then either just stay on the road or, to save your studs and knees, pick up the path that runs parallel to it. After about 700m you'll be back at your starting point.

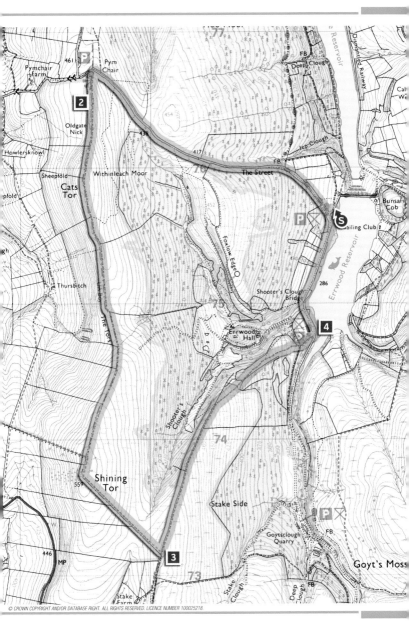

10.5km

INTRODUCTION

A fantastic trail run, always interesting and varied enough to make it a firm favourite. The hill is hard work, but well worth the effort! A top tip for this run is not to be lured into setting out too fast, just because you are surrounded by herds of tourists visiting the house. Save a little bit for the return leg, you don't want any kids overtaking you as you struggle in over the last kilometre. Being from Yorkshire I only ever pay for an hour in the car park as well, which sets a bit of a challenge.

THE ROUTE

This route starts from the lovely village of Baslow – dare you only pay for one hour's parking? The first four or five kilometres are a delight on fast trails alongside the River Derwent, before the route turns mean, with a hard tarmac climb up Beeley Lane and then a moorland trail up to the escarpment of Rabbit Warren. Then it's back to the fast running once more as the route leads back to Chatsworth House, into fine parkland (look out for the deer) and so to the car.

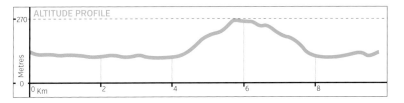

≫ CHATSWORTH

DISTANCE 10.5KM ≫ **ASCENT** 250M ≫ **MAX ALTITUDE** 270M ≫ **TYPICAL TIME** 1–1:30 HRS
≫ **TERRAIN** GOOD TRAILS, SOME TARMAC, MOSTLY WELL DRAINED, WITH ONE SHORT STEEP PATH SECTION
≫ **NAVIGATION** STRAIGHTFORWARD ON GOOD TRAILS ≫ **START/FINISH** BASLOW PAY AND DISPLAY
CAR PARK ≫ **GRID REF** SK 257721 ≫ **SATNAV** DE45 1SR ≫ **OS MAP** EXPLORER OL24 THE PEAK DISTRICT
– WHITE PEAK AREA ≫ **REFRESHMENTS** CHARLIE'S, BASLOW TEL: 01246 582 619

DIRECTIONS » CHATSWORTH

S   Leave the car park and **turn immediately right** down the road. Cross the bridge and **turn right** down the lane alongside the river. The lane soon narrows to a path after the gate. Ignore the footpath branching off on the right and **continue straight on** to the revolving gate. Go through this and start the fast section of this run proper. The path continues flat, soon turning to tarmac through the parkland, past all manner of cottages, cricket pitches, stately trees and assorted things that you buy for a Duke who has everything. **Staying straight on**, keeping the River Derwent on your right, the track meets the road heading up to the house at a bridge. **Turn right** across the bridge, then **turn left** to pick up the smaller path running downstream with the Derwent now on your left.

2   Follow the path, with a few choices depending on whether you want to run straight or follow the sweep of the river. Eventually, after another couple of kilometres of fine running, you meet another road by a bridge. Go through the stile, on to the road and **turn left** across the bridge. (A perfectly good 'flat 10k' simply returns the way you have come from this point.) After crossing the bridge, follow the road to the bend and **take the left fork**. Follow the lane, soon becoming steep/very steep. After a large farm on the right, look out for a permissive footpath on the **left**. **Take this**, heading uphill on to the moorland above the Chatsworth Estate. Once on the top of the edge, the path meets a good track. **Turn left** and follow this until you meet a T-junction of good tracks.

3   **Turn left** and follow the track. After the first switchback look out for a path leaving the track downhill. Take this and it soon picks up and runs parallel to the lane, re-joining it after some distance. Stay on the tarmac lane and follow it into the back of the Chatsworth House grounds, near the farm/adventure playground. Continue downhill into the car parks on the right and drop down through these, picking up a road **on the right** leaving the bottom of the car parks (not the one that heads uphill!). Follow this, parallel to but some way above the river, and after about 1.5km – just before the larger stand of trees – **head left**, across the meadow, to re-join the start of the run at the revolving gate. Jog gently back to the car park.

NIK AND LISSA COOK ROCK HOPPING ABOVE WINDGATHER

INTRODUCTION

A route that genuinely has a bit of everything: farmland, forests, a stunning ridgeline, open moors, rock outcrops and reservoir-side trails. There's lots of climbing in the first half of the run but you're rewarded by some great views, plenty of descending and a lovely flattish run in to the finish.

THE ROUTE

Leaving the glamorous lay-by start, there's a short downhill before a steep climb through the tiny village of Taxal and on to the stunning Taxal Moor. You gain height steadily on the ridge before plunging into woodland and ascending once again to the top of the popular climbing crag, Windgather Rocks. The clue's in the name, so pack a decent windproof. Heading across the moors, you're still gaining height, but gently and you need to watch out for deep bogs! Just below Pym Chair you have the option of tacking on the Shining Tor route (16.8km total, page 37) if you fancy a longer run. If not, the downhill fun starts now. Hop from rut to rut down The Street and then let loose and plunge through the trees, praying your studs grip, to Fernilee Reservoir. Run off the lactic burn on the undulating trail alongside the reservoir before heading into the picturesque Goyt Valley. Don't forget to save a bit for the cruel finishing climb or, if the weather's good, to have a paddle in the ford.

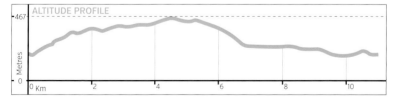

≫ WINDGATHER ROCKS

DISTANCE 11KM ≫ **ASCENT** 320M ≫ **MAX ALTITUDE** 467M ≫ **TYPICAL TIME** 1–2 HRS ≫ **TERRAIN** MIXED, WITH SOME BOGGY GROUND AND STEEP SLIPPERY DESCENTS IN THE WET ≫ **NAVIGATION** MOSTLY EASY CLEAR FOOTPATHS BUT SOME FIDDLY BITS ≫ **START/FINISH** LARGE LAY-BY ON LONG HILL (A5004) JUST OUTSIDE OF WHALEY BRIDGE ≫ **GRID REF** SK 008798 ≫ **SATNAV** SK23 7EY (NEAREST) ≫ **OS MAP** EXPLORER OL24 THE PEAK DISTRICT – WHITE PEAK AREA ≫ **REFRESHMENTS** MOBILE CATERING VAN IN LAY-BY

DIRECTIONS ≫ WINDGATHER ROCKS

S   Find the path that leads west down from the car park — cross the river by the footbridge or ford and then climb steeply on the narrow tarmac path. At the top, **turn left** on the road and, after about 50m, pick up the footpath off to your **right**. Follow the footpath up though the fields, keeping an eye out for the two ladder stiles.

2   Come out on Taxal Moor Road. **Turn left** and follow the road for a couple of hundred metres. Take the footpath off to your **right** and begin the climb up on to Taxal Moor. You'll pass a sign indicating you're heading the right way. Eventually you'll come to a wall. Ignore the footpath through the gate but instead follow the obvious trod off to your **left** up the short rise. Follow this path, keeping the wall on your right. As you start to head downhill, **turn right** down a steep descent, **left** when you come to the wall and then go over the ladder stile. Follow the path into the wood and then **bear left**, descending steeply and then climbing even more steeply out the other side. Come to a wall at the top, **turn left**, go over a stile and follow the path. **Turn right** hugging the wall and then **left** to bring you out on the top of Windgather Rocks.

3   Run south along the top of the crag, past the smaller quarry, and then, via a gate, pick up the path that runs parallel to the road. Enjoy the moorland trail, watch out for the bogs and, after about 1km, follow a **left hand fork** and cross a small footbridge. Stay on this path until you come to the road. **Turn left** and follow the path that runs parallel to the road downhill. After 1.5km, the road veers to the right but you want to **turn left** through the gate that goes on to a broad forest track.

4   Immediately on your **right** as you go through the gate is a footpath signed to *Fernilee Reservoir*. Follow this path, **turning right** after the first 50m, and enjoy the steep descent through the forest to the side of the reservoir. **Turn left** on to the main path and head north, running the length of the reservoir on the undulating path.

Directions continue on page 50.

5   At the far end of the reservoir, you'll come to a metalled track – follow this round to the **right**. After 150m **turn left** on to another track and follow this for 800m. **Turn right** going through a farm gate, pass in front of the farm cottage (watch out for the slippery flagstones) and pick up the path that drops away to your **left**. Follow this path downhill, cross one footbridge and then watch out for and cross another one on your **right**. At the end of the bridge, **turn left** and follow the path through the fields, keeping the river to your left. Stay on this path that bears round to the left, into Shallcross Woods, signed to Taxal.

6   Eventually you'll go through a gate and find yourself just above the ford and footbridge you crossed at the beginning of the run. **Head right** up the steep nasty kick and pop out in the car park. Treat yourself to a bacon butty and a cup of tea from the mobile catering van.

12 » MACCLESFIELD FOREST & WILDBOARCLOUGH

11.1km

INTRODUCTION

Starting and finishing at the second highest pub in England, there's a real sense of wild remoteness to these moors. This is a great run with the unusual bonus of a flat and downhill start to get warmed up on. There's plenty of climbing to come though and, with some challenging technical conditions underfoot, don't expect to set any PBs.

THE ROUTE

Leaving the pub and the notorious A537 (named the UK's most dangerous road in 2003), you gently gain the 20 metres of height on a broad bridleway that takes you to the 'summit' of the run. You then drop rapidly, following the course of the clough, hopping from rock to rock and avoiding the sucking boggy patches. Then the

inevitable climbing begins. It's almost unnoticeable to begin with, but eventually the unmistakable shape of Shutlingsloe hill looms and the work begins. The lower flanks are testing but the final section is an absolute hands-on-knees brute. A stone-flagged descent drops into Macclesfield Forest, from where you begin the long climb home. It's never too steep but, with the best part of two kilometres uphill, measure your effort. Eventually, after some great singletrack running, you're spat out on to the A537. A little detour saves you a stretch on the road and carries you back to your car. If you want a longer run, link this route to Shining Tor and Windgather Rocks (pages 37 and 47) for an extremely enjoyable and varied 29.5-kilometre jaunt.

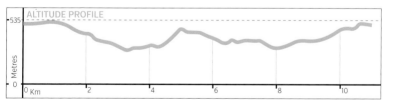

ALTITUDE PROFILE

» MACCLESFIELD FOREST & WILDBOARCLOUGH

DISTANCE 11.1KM » *ASCENT* 431M » *MAX ALTITUDE* 535M » *TYPICAL TIME* 1:15–2:15 HRS » *TERRAIN* MIXED INCLUDING SOME ROCKY STRETCHES » *NAVIGATION* CLEAR FOOTPATHS » *START/FINISH* CAT AND FIDDLE INN » *GRID REF* SK 001718 » *SATNAV* SK11 0AR » *OS MAP* EXPLORER OL24 THE PEAK DISTRICT – WHITE PEAK AREA » *REFRESHMENTS* CAT AND FIDDLE INN TEL: 01298 78 366

DIRECTIONS » MACCLESFIELD FOREST & WILDBOARCLOUGH

S Pick up the bridleway that starts almost directly opposite the pub. Follow it for about a kilometre before taking a footpath off to the **right** signposted *Cumberland Brook and Wildboarclough*. After about 400m it drops sharply left and then follows the course of the clough. You'll come to a junction of tracks. Take the wide track that goes off to the **right** through the gate. Follow this rough, rocky and rooty track downhill, **go left** over a footbridge and eventually come to a road.

2 **Go straight across** the road into the farmyard and find the footpath at the far **left-hand** corner. Cross the field, over another footbridge and come to another road. **Turn left** and follow the road briefly before taking the footpath signed off to the **right**. Follow this obvious path for about 500m. Take the metalled track marked as a footpath to your **right**. Just before the track goes through the farm gates, take the footpath to your **left** heading towards the obvious summit of Shutlingsloe. Follow the main well-worn path straight up, through the rocks and to the trig point.

3 At the summit, take the steeply descending flagged path off to the **right**, go over the stile and follow the flags that run parallel to the wall. After 200m go through the gate on your **left** and follow the path over the fields to another gate on the treeline of the forest. Follow the path **straight on** and come out on to the main forest trail. **Turn right** and follow the trail for just over 1km until you come to a road.

4 **Turn right** on the road and go steeply downhill for 300m. At the bottom **turn left**, **then right**, and then pick up the metalled track running north-east that's marked as a footpath. Follow this well-marked path for about 1km. There are a few kinks and kicks but it generally keeps heading in the same direction and is easy to follow. Eventually, within sight of a farm, you'll come across a sign displaying information and the direction of the concessionary path you need to follow. Drop down to the **right** to pick up the path and follow the white markers. Keep following the clear path and markers uphill and the path will bring you out on to the A537.

5 Cross the road and go up the entrance way to the tearooms. Take the footpath off to your **right**. Follow the track that cuts across the bend in the top of the road. (If you're adding on the Shining Tor and/or Windgather Rocks route take either of the footpaths off to your **left** to return you to those routes.) If not, come out on to the road, **turn left** and run the final couple of hundred metres on the verge back to the pub.

BECKY LOUNDS AND KEITH SHARPLES IN CHEE DALE

INTRODUCTION

You've got a bit of everything on this route. A disused railway line, a grassy switchback climb, a road section to open up on, fast technical descents and one of the most atmospheric and challenging paths we've ever run.

THE ROUTE

Head west on the Monsal Trail towards Chee Dale. After just under three kilometres on the trail, pick up the signs for the Pennine Bridleway and climb northwards up the steep grassy switchbacks. Stay on the Pennine Bridleway, making the most of some fast downhill tarmac and then, just before Tunstead, turn right on to a walled farm track. After a brief section of road in Wormhill, enjoy a fast descent that finishes with a fantastic steep grassy plummet into Monk's Dale. It all gets a little surreal and slightly Tolkien-esque as you then pick your way along the moss covered and limestone strewn trail. It's certainly not the fastest running and you'll probably slip and slide a bit, but it's truly a magical place. Finish with a steep climb back up to the Monsal Trail and the car.

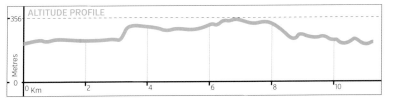

>> MILLER'S DALE

DISTANCE 11.3KM >> **ASCENT** 231M >> **MAX ALTITUDE** 356M >> **TYPICAL TIME** 0:50-2:00 HRS >> **TERRAIN** WELL-SURFACED TRACKS, SOME TARMAC (SORRY!) AND SOME SUPER-SLIPPERY LIMESTONE >> **NAVIGATION** ALL ON EASY TO FOLLOW TRAILS WITH A LARGE PROPORTION ON WAYMARKED PENNINE BRIDLEWAY >> **START/FINISH** MONSAL TRAIL STATION CAR PARK, MILLER'S DALE >> **GRID REF** SK 138732 >> **SATNAV** SK17 8SN >> **OS MAP** EXPLORER OL24 THE PEAK DISTRICT – WHITE PEAK AREA >> **REFRESHMENTS** SNACK VAN IN CAR PARK; ANGLER'S REST, MILLER'S DALE TEL: 01298 871 323

DIRECTIONS » MILLER'S DALE

S   **Turn right** (west) on the Monsal Trail and head towards Chee Dale. After about 1km, you'll enter the Chee Tor Tunnels. They're not marked on older OS maps as the tunnels on the Monsal Trail have only recently reopened.

2   Emerge from the next tunnel (Rusher Cutting Tunnel) and, after approximately 700m, just after a large viaduct, pick up the National Trail signs for the Pennine Bridleway heading north towards Tunstead and Wormhill.

3   Climb the steep switchbacks and, at the top, keep following the *Pennine Bridleway* signs through a farm and on to a metalled road. Stay on the road, descending steadily and, just before you come into Tunstead, keep an eye out for the Pennine Bridleway sign indicating you to take the track off to the **right**.

4   Follow the track, which opens out on to a grassy flank. Go through a farm and then **turn right** on to the road into Wormhill. Almost immediately, **turn left** off the road, marked as *Pennine Bridleway* and follow the track.

5   After a left kink, the track narrows and begins to descend steeply. It then opens on to a field and steepens more. The Pennine Bridleway contours across to your left but you want to **keep heading straight down**. Follow this footpath all the way along Monk's Dale and into Miller's Dale. Emerge by the side of the church, cross on to the minor road opposite (signed *Litton Mill (only)*), take the footpath on the right after 50m. Climb steeply to the Monsal Trail and **turn right** back to Miller's Dale station.

THE MONSAL TRAIL THROUGH CHEE DALE

14 ≫ CARSINGTON LOOP   12.3km

INTRODUCTION

An ideal 'trail' run for novices, road runners wanting to try 'soft-roading', or a fast paced training loop without navigational issues or technical terrain to distract you. Pleasantly varied with plenty to see and finishing along the top of the dam wall is brilliant. Don't think it's dead flat though – the middle third is fairly lumpy.

THE ROUTE

Follow the fully waymarked path all around the Carsington Water reservoir. It's signed clockwise, but is easy to follow in either direction. There are a number of sections where the bike and foot loop diverge but they always meet up again. There's also an option for a flatter trail that hugs the waterline more closely and, if you want to take this, the points where it branches off are clearly marked.

DIRECTIONS ≫ CARSINGTON LOOP

S Pick up the trail at the north-western corner of the car park and follow the footprint markings and clear fingerposts clockwise around the loop. It really is that easy.

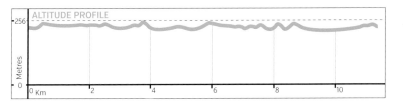

ALTITUDE PROFILE

256

Metres

0   0 Km   2   4   6   8   10

≫ CARSINGTON LOOP

DISTANCE 12.3KM ≫ **ASCENT** 165M ≫ **MAX ALTITUDE** 256M ≫ **TYPICAL TIME** 0:50–1:30 HRS ≫ **TERRAIN** ALMOST ALL ON WELL-MAINTAINED TRAILS, BUT OCCASIONAL MUDDY PATCH IN WET ≫ **NAVIGATION** GUARANTEED 100% IDIOTPROOF ≫ **START/FINISH** CARSINGTON WATER VISITOR CENTRE ≫ **GRID REF** SK 240516 ≫ **SATNAV** DE6 1ST ≫ **OS MAP** EXPLORER OL24 THE PEAK DISTRICT – WHITE PEAK AREA ≫ **REFRESHMENTS** CAFE AND RESTAURANT IN VISITOR CENTRE

IAN WINTERBURN LEAVING THE SUMMIT OF BLACK HILL

15 >> BLACK HILL & LADDOW ROCKS   13.4km

INTRODUCTION

The most northerly run in this book, taking in the summit of Black Hill. Expect some bog trotting in all but the driest conditions and, if you take it on in the wet, prepare for some peaty fun and low average speeds. Run it either clockwise or anti-clockwise depending on whether you'd prefer to climb or descend on the flagstones of the Pennine Way. We've described it anti-clockwise.

THE ROUTE

After a very brief warm-up on tarmac, you soon turn on to the moors and start climbing. If it's a clear day, you can look back across the valley and see your return route. You're soon on to bleak and atmospheric moorland and trying to pick the best route through the bogs. A steep kick takes you on to Westend Moss and White Low from where you can see the Holme Moss TV transmission station. On the flatter moor top, you can let your stride open out, enjoy the soft yielding surface and try to leap the bogs. As you get nearer to the summit, the path becomes less clear and you'll have to negotiate some classic hags, groughs and shoe-sucking bogs. Tick the summit and then begin the fast homeward charge, first down the love-them-or-hate-them flag-stones, then on to some brilliant technical trails past Laddow Rocks and finally back to Crowden.

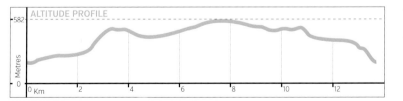

>> BLACK HILL & LADDOW ROCKS

DISTANCE 13.4KM >> *ASCENT* 455M >> *MAX ALTITUDE* 582M >> *TYPICAL TIME* 1:30–3:00 HRS >> *TERRAIN* BOG, FLAGSTONES AND ROCKY PATHS >> *NAVIGATION* THE STRETCH TO THE SUMMIT OF BLACK HILL CAN BE TRICKY SO MAKE SURE YOU'VE GOT A MAP AND COMPASS >> *START/FINISH* CROWDEN CAR PARK >> *GRID REF* SK 072993 >> *SATNAV* SK13 1HZ >> *OS MAP* EXPLORER OL1 THE PEAK DISTRICT – DARK PEAK AREA >> *REFRESHMENTS* NOT A LOT AROUND HERE

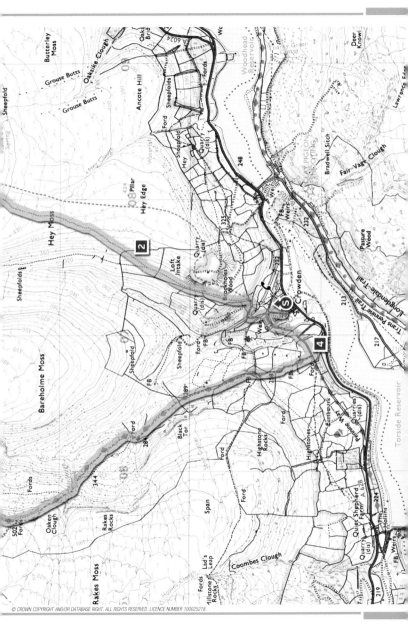

S Walk to the toilet block and **turn right** up the walled lane. **Straight across** at the crossroads, following the metalled track away from the youth hostel, bear sharply round to the **right** and then, on the apex of a sharp left hand bend, take the footpath off to the **left**. Gain height and follow this footpath, making sure you take the **right fork** after about 1km. This will keep you climbing and heading slightly off to the east.

2 Follow this path that occasionally becomes slightly vague and has a number of trods criss-crossing but generally keep heading in the same direction. After the steeper section on to Westend Moss, the path bears fairly sharply east before returning north and then slightly west.

3 **Keep heading north-west** to the summit of Black Hill. Leave the hill on the Pennine Way. If the visibility is poor – whether running the route in either direction, but especially if you're going clockwise – you should take a bearing leaving the summit. Once you hit the flagstones, the Pennine Way is easy to follow and you stick to it almost all the way back.

4 Just as you reach Crowden, you'll come to a T-junction. **Turn left** in the opposite direction to the Pennine Way and right at the crossroads back to the car park.

16 >> STANAGE   13.5km

INTRODUCTION

A challenging run despite having really only one hill climb of note. The terrain is beautiful, and while some sections feel remote you are never that far from the crowds. The route is exposed, never really dropping below 400 metres.

THE ROUTE

The route starts along the top of Burbage North edge before heading out across the moor to the wide and sandy Houndkirk Roman Road. Passing beneath the Ox Stones, it heads back up to the road, crossing it and heading up Rud Hill on often-wet grassy trails. The run now breaks out over the moor on undefined and usually boggy ground as it crosses to White Stones and drops to Redmires Reservoir. A good, honest climb up the big wide track to Stanedge Pole brings one to a tough and rocky bit of running along the top of Stanage Edge and then a pleasant sprint back down to the start.

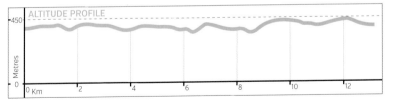

ALTITUDE PROFILE

>> STANAGE

DISTANCE 13.5KM >> *ASCENT* 260M >> *MAX ALTITUDE* 450M >> *TYPICAL TIME* 1:30 HRS >> *TERRAIN* MIXED, MANY TOUGH SECTIONS, BOGGY, ROCKY WITH A FEW FAST STRETCHES >> *NAVIGATION* MOSTLY EASY ALTHOUGH NOT ALL ON OBVIOUS PATHS >> *START/FINISH* LARGE LAY-BY OR CAR PARK AT BURBAGE BRIDGE >> *GRID REF* SK 260830 >> *SATNAV* S11 7TS (NEAREST) >> *OS MAP* EXPLORER OL1 THE PEAK DISTRICT – DARK PEAK AREA >> *REFRESHMENTS* NORFOLK ARMS, RINGINGLOW TEL: 0114 230 2197

DIRECTIONS >> STANAGE

S   From the lay-by to the east of the bridge, squeeze through the tiny gate at the far end and head on to the top of the edge. Run along the edge, which is rocky and boggy in equal measure. After around 1.5km the path drops towards a cairn – **take the path left**, uphill, towards a second cairn and heading out on to the moor.

2   Follow the path to a gate. Go through this, and keeping the fence on your left, follow the path to a second gate. Go through this on to the unsurfaced sandy Houndkirk Road. **Turn left**, eventually climbing up and over the brow and dropping to an obvious crossroads of tracks after 1.5km. **Turn left**, uphill. Follow the track to a gate at the road. Go through the small gate on the right, **straight across the road** through a stile and out once again on to moorland trail.

3   Drop down over boggy ground and then climb, keeping more or less **straight ahead** and ignoring turnings. Navigate straight on through the small quarries, heading towards the farm. The path drops into a walled sunken lane. Follow this to and through the farmyard, down the farm track and on to the road.

4   **Turn left** on to the road, and then after a short distance go **straight ahead/left** over the stile on to the permissive footpath. Follow the track up to a stile and into a field. Keeping the wall to your left, go up through the field and over the next stile and out on to open moorland.

5   The trail is usually quite boggy and ill-defined in places. Keep **straight ahead** as best you can, never losing height, until the ground becomes properly rocky – this is White Stones. When the rocks become refrigerator-sized look for the trail heading downhill to the **right**. Follow this towards the head of the reservoirs. As you join the wide track, **turn left** through a gate on to a good uphill track.

6   Follow the track uphill, eventually emerging on to open moorland. **Keep straight ahead** past the distinctive Stanedge Pole until the track swings right near the top of Stanage Edge. **Take the footpath on the left**, **keeping left** as you reach the edge itself, and follow the always-rocky track along the top. Eventually climb uphill, passing a trig point on your right, and go over the brow. As the path peters out, head along a short flagged section, heading pleasantly and quickly back to the road. A short hop along tarmac and there you go: you've done another run.

17 » HOPE VALLEY TRAIN RUNS: EDALE TO CHINLEY

14.2km

INTRODUCTION

Sometimes it's a motivating change to run A to B rather than a loop and the Sheffield to Manchester train line along the Hope Valley opens up numerous options for runners. With a map, a train timetable and a little imagination, some of the best running in the Peak is opened up. This is a personal favourite, returning to my (Nik's!) home village of Chinley from Edale over Kinder and with a bit of bonus climbing thrown in at the end. It's an eight-minute train journey through the Cowburn Tunnel but the run will take you a bit longer.

THE ROUTE

Having left the station, trot up into Edale and pick up the Pennine Way. You soon turn off this, on to a wonderful contouring path and eventually drop into Crowden Clough. Enjoy the rock hopping at the bottom and a fun bit of scrambling near the top. It's not the quickest way up on to the Kinder plateau but it's definitely one of the most entertaining. You're now on the plateau to Edale Rocks, but lose height rapidly and hurtle down in the direction of Hayfield and then carry on descending to the bottom of Dimpus Clough. There's a monster climb out, with a short moment to catch your breath on the Pennine Bridleway before tackling South Head. More fast and fun descending follows and takes you into Chinley, hopefully in time for your return train.

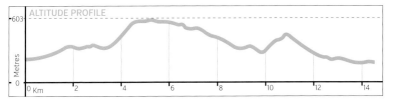

ALTITUDE PROFILE

603 — Metres — 0

0 Km   2   4   6   8   10   12   14

» HOPE VALLEY TRAIN RUNS: EDALE TO CHINLEY

DISTANCE 14.2KM » *ASCENT* 629M » *MAX ALTITUDE* 603M » *TYPICAL TIME* 1:30-3:30 HRS » *TERRAIN* THE ROUTE INCLUDES SOME SCRAMBLING AND CHALLENGING FELL TERRAIN » *NAVIGATION* CAN BE TRICKY IN THE CLOUD SO TAKE (AND KNOW HOW TO USE) A MAP AND COMPASS » *START/FINISH* EDALE TRAIN STATION/CHINLEY TRAIN STATION » *GRID REF* SK 122853 (EDALE) TO SK 037825 (CHINLEY) » *SATNAV* S36 4GY (EDALE) » *OS MAP* EXPLORER OL1 THE PEAK DISTRICT – DARK PEAK AREA » *REFRESHMENTS* PENNY POT CAFE, EDALE TEL: 01433 670 293

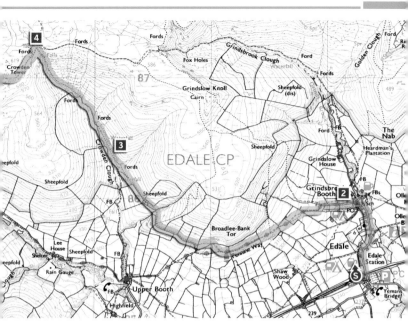

DIRECTIONS ≫ HOPE VALLEY TRAIN RUNS: EDALE TO CHINLEY

S **Turn left** out of the station access road and follow the lane uphill into Edale village, passing the Moorland Centre on your right. Just after the village shop on your left, **turn left** on to the Pennine Way.

2 Follow the path through a narrow avenue of trees and then go through the gate. Keep following the flagstones, go through a couple of sets of gates but then look for an Access Land notice and a gate 50m or so to the **right** of the main path. Go through this gate and follow the obvious path that contours along the flank of the hill. (If you miss this turn and end up in Upper Booth, take the **signed right turn** to *Crowden Clough* just after the village.) If you're on the correct path, you'll drop down, cross a small stream, climb briefly and pass a wood on your left before descending into the main clough.

Directions continue overleaf

3 Pick your way up the clough. There are a number of trods but, if you stick closely to the water and keep heading up, you can't go wrong. There's a bit of scrambling to do near the top before you pop out on to the main east–west path along the southern edge of Kinder.

4 **Turn left**, climb a short steep rise and then follow the path past the Wool Packs, Pym Chair and Noe Stool. Drop down past Swine's Back, pick up the flagstones and drop to a wide track. **Turn right**, pass Edale Cross and descend Oaken Clough. Enjoy the fast, rocky and technical downhill but take care not to miss the footpath off to the **left** signposted *Dimpus Clough*. It's just after a gate, so you shouldn't be going too fast.

5 Follow the path, crossing a couple of fields and then dropping steeply to the clough. Climb out steeply, then, heading almost due south, run to the Pennine Bridleway. Cross the bridleway and climb steeply up to the summit of South Head.

6 Follow the marked concessionary path down the southerly ridge of South Head. Eventually you'll come to a fingerpost, **turn right** and carry on descending over two stiles and on to a semi-metalled road. **Turn left** and, about 200m after a cattle grid, take the footpath off to the **right** down across another field. Follow a tight little path through the properties and then briefly climb up to the A624 Hayfield Road.

7 **Take the track directly opposite** and then, after about 25m, take a footpath off to your **left** through a small gate. Follow the footpath across fields, cross a footbridge over the railway and come out on to the B6062. **Turn right** and follow the road into Chinley, and the station.

DESCENDING TOWARDS EDALE CROSS

DESCENDING CHINLEY CHURN

INTRODUCTION

Like all perfect runs, this finishes at an award-winning pub where muddy runners are more than welcome. Centering around Chinley village, it takes in three local summits, along with a 'near miss' on Chinley Churn, where there isn't access to the very top. Never straying far from civilisation, this run is an ideal stepping stone to committing and exposed routes. You get a real sense of wilderness and technical terrain to contend with, but beating a retreat is always easy enough.

THE ROUTE

The run starts with an easy tarmac warm-up before heading towards the obvious and imposing peak of South Head. There's a bit of fiddly route finding but, once on the path up the obvious south ridge of the hill, the only way is up. At the top, take a moment to admire the views over Kinder before plummeting down the fast descent to the Pennine Bridleway and heading straight up the grassy climb to the spectacular Mount Famine ridge. A steep and rocky descent spits you back out towards the wide, well-surfaced trail that grinds up towards Cracken Edge. Use your time here to refuel before climbing the narrow trod to the obvious and imaginatively-named rock buttress, Big Stone. Then enjoy the technical, mostly flat and downhill running – including a mildly vertiginous goat track – through old quarry workings and tackle a short road climb before a blisteringly fast grassy descent to the village of Buxworth. You now follow the Eccles Pike Fell Race route, which includes two brutal climbs, before finally dropping off the hill on another super-fast descent, crossing the A6 and running back into Whitehough.

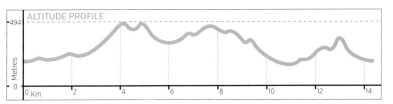

ALTITUDE PROFILE

494

Metres

0

0 Km   2   4   6   8   10   12   14

>> **CHINLEY SKYLINE**

DISTANCE 14.7KM >> **ASCENT** 790M >> **MAX ALTITUDE** 494M >> **TYPICAL TIME** 2–3 HRS >> **TERRAIN** ROUGH TRAILS AND FOOTPATHS, INCLUDING SOME STEEP CLIMBS AND DESCENTS >> **NAVIGATION** MOSTLY CLEAR PATHS BUT COMPETENCE WITH MAP AND COMPASS NEEDED IF CLOUD COMES DOWN >> **START/FINISH** THE OLD HALL INN, WHITEHOUGH >> **GRID REF** SK 039821 >> **SATNAV** SK23 6EJ >> **OS MAP** EXPLORER OL1 THE PEAK DISTRICT – DARK PEAK AREA >> **REFRESHMENTS** THE OLD HALL INN TEL: 01663 750 529

THE FINAL SUMMIT, ECCLES PIKE

DIRECTIONS ≫ CHINLEY SKYLINE

S From the pub, run down the hill, over a humpbacked bridge and then up into Chinley. **Carry straight on**, pass the post office on your right, and then follow the B6062 round to the right. After about 800m, take the footpath off to your **left**, cross the railway and head across the fields towards White Knowl Farm. Go through the small gate, **turn right** on the track and **go straight across** the A624.

2 Run down the metalled road for 50m and just before the gate to East Meats, **turn right** down some steps and follow the path between the buildings before clambering over a stone stile. Head across the bottom of the field, cross into the next and then bear towards the top right corner where you'll find a gate. **Turn left** on the semi-metalled road, run over the cattle grid and, after about 100m, **turn right** over a stile.

3 Head straight up the steep field, over another stile, follow the wall straight on and you'll find a fingerpost. **Turn left** and follow the permissive path up South Head. Keep a sharp look out for the various markers but the path fundamentally sticks to the obvious ridge.

4 At the summit, **turn left**, drop down to and cross the Pennine Bridleway and head up the obvious flank of Mount Famine. Follow the path along the ridge and keep to the **left** as it starts to descend. Take care on the final steep and rocky descent before continuing across a field and then **bearing left** to go over a ladder stile. **Turn left** through the gate and pick up the Pennine Bridleway. Go through two gates and, at the second, leave the Pennine Bridleway, cross the wide track and take the track opposite that'll take you back to the A624.

5 Cross the main road, **turn left** and then take the first turning on the **right**. Pass Peep O Day farm on your right, go through the gate and follow the main track uphill. Keep climbing, follow the track round to the **left** and at the bottom of the descent, take the footpath through the gate to your **left**. Follow this track up past the derelict barn and stick to it until you see the obvious trod off to **your right** up to Big Stone.

6   At Big Stone, **turn left** and follow the grassy trail heading south. Cross a stone stile, **turn left** and drop down to the main path in front of the old quarry workings. When you hit the path **turn right** and follow it down the eroded goat track (watch your footing) past the old pulley. Bear round to the **right**, go over a stile and enjoy the fast and fun trail that, after two more stiles, spits you out on to Over Hill Road. **Turn right** and climb steeply on the road for about 150m and then, as the road goes round to the right, take the footpath through the gate on your **left**.

7   Drop down through the fields to Cotebank Farm and follow the path down the slippery stone flagged steps, through the garden and past the flagpole. Head on to the road and go **straight over** the stone stile immediately opposite you next to the farm gate. Go down through the field, keeping the double parallel walls to your left. Keep on the path and you'll come out on to the B6062. **Turn right** and follow the road under a bridge and then down a short hill.

8   Just after passing the school on your left, take the road on your **left** and continue down to the canal basin and pass the Navigation Pub on your left. Keep following the road, it crosses over the A6 and then bends round to the left. Keep following it, ignoring the Silk Hill turning and, just before you get to the playing fields, take the small road off to your **right**. This climbs steeply and then narrows down to a path before you come to a gate.

9   Go through the gate, **turn left**, keep the wall to your right and follow the trod across the field heading south-east. In the bottom left corner of the field you'll find a stile. Cross it and then **head straight up** the next field following the yellow posts. At the top of the field, go over a stone stile, cross the road and take the footpath opposite.

10 **Fork right** and follow this path for about 400m before going over another stile. About 10m after the stile, **turn sharply right** and follow the path straight up the side of the hill. Pass the copse of conifers on your left and then **bear left** to the summit of Eccles Pike. Go straight down the wide grassy track heading east, take the **sharp left** switchback at the bottom and then take the byway off to the **right**. Follow this down to the road, **turn right** and then, at the T-junction, **turn left** and romp down the hill back into Whitehough and a well-deserved pint.

SARAH AND TONY WHITEHOUSE HEADING UP WILLIAM CLOUGH

INTRODUCTION

On 24 April 1932, 400 hikers gathered in Bowden Bridge Quarry, listened to a rousing speech by Benny Rothman and then walked illegally up on to Kinder. This, the event now celebrated as the Kinder Mass Trespass, was the first step in securing the access rights we have today. The run here on Kinder has a bit of everything, open moorland, fast single-track, scrambles, rock hopping and fast descents, making it a Dark Peak classic.

THE ROUTE

From the quarry, head towards Hayfield, turning on to the Snake Path. You're now on the route of the Kinder Downfall fell race. The grassy pastures become wilder as you gain height, and soon you're on to the open moors. A fast traverse of White Brow and a steep technical descent spit you out at the bottom of William Clough. The climb from here is long, but thinking about the

best line occupies your mind. Eventually it steepens and, after some rough steps, you leave the Clough and hit the Pennine Way. Catch your breath before your last significant climb of the day, up Ashop Head. It's a steep rocky tester but, with it conquered, you're on the Kinder Plateau, where the running is fairly flat but finding a rhythm is tough. On a day when the cloud's down, you'll hear the Downfall before you see it. If the wind's blowing right, you might even see it 'up-falling'.

Carry on along the Pennine Way, soon leaving the race route and heading on to Kinderlow End. On a clear day the views are amazing and, if the clag is down, you've got the historical interest of the tumulus. A steep down-scramble loses height quickly and, if you've still got strength in your legs, it's fast running and obvious route finding back towards civilisation. With about a kilometre to go, you hit tarmac, giving the perfect cool down.

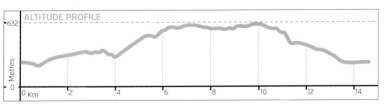

ALTITUDE PROFILE

≫ **KINDER DOWNFALL FROM HAYFIELD**

DISTANCE 15KM ≫ **ASCENT** 690M ≫ **MAX ALTITUDE** 632M ≫ **TYPICAL TIME** 1.5–2.5 HRS ≫ **TERRAIN** ROUGH AND ROCKY HIGH MOORLAND ≫ **NAVIGATION** MOSTLY OBVIOUS PATHS AND BRIDLEWAYS BUT COMPETENCE WITH MAP AND COMPASS IS NEEDED ≫ **START/FINISH** BOWDEN BRIDGE CAR PARK ≫ **GRID REF** SK 048869 ≫ **SATNAV** SK22 2LE ≫ **OS MAP** EXPLORER OL1 THE PEAK DISTRICT – DARK PEAK AREA ≫ **REFRESHMENTS** ROSIE'S CAFE IN HAYFIELD TEL: 01663 745 597

KINDER DOWNFALL

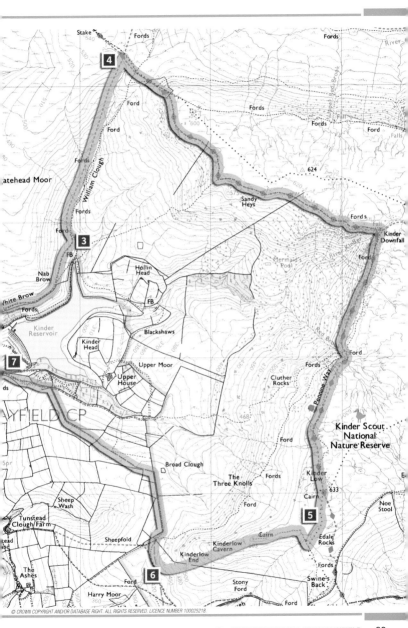

DIRECTIONS ≫ KINDER DOWNFALL FROM HAYFIELD

S Out of the car park, **turn right** and head up the gentle hill back towards Hayfield. Pass The Sportsman pub on your right and, after about 800m, **turn right** off the road on to the signposted *Snake Path*. Stay on this path though a number of gates, gaining height and heading towards Middle Moor.

2 At the Shooting Cabin, **bear right** and then stick to the **upper left-hand footpath**. Follow the singletrack footpath across the slopes of White Brow. Stay on this path and then descend off to the **right** and come to the bottom of William Clough.

3 Follow the Clough upwards. Climb out of the Clough by some steep rough steps and come to a broad obvious track. Follow the track in the same direction you've been travelling and you'll come to a Pennine Way fingerpost.

4 **Turn right** and head up Ashop Head. Once at the top follow the cairns and well-worn path of the Pennine Way. Go past the Downfall, past Red Brook and past Kinder Low trig point.

5 After the trig point, you'll come across a flagged path that, after a short while, forks. Take the **right hand fork** and head towards Kinderlow End. Pass the tumulus, leave the flagstones and follow the broad grassy path. The ground then steepens. Scramble down and come to the bridleway at the bottom.

6 **Turn right** and follow the bridleway. At its end, **turn left** through a gate and then follow the grassy bridleway across fields before **bearing right** and descending to the edge of a wood by the side of the reservoir. Stay on the bridleway, **turn left** and descend to the gate.

7 **Turn left** on the road, follow it downhill for about 1km back to the car park.

VARIED RUNNING ON THE KINDER PLATEAU

STEVE FRANKLIN IN DOVE DALE

INTRODUCTION

Definitely a trail rather than fell route, this White Peak run utilises the converted railway line of the Tissington Trail to allow a stunning south to north passage of the spectacular Dove Dale. Caves, limestone spires, rising trout and the burbling of the River Dove distract you from the steady but constant climb. Save something in your legs for the inevitable burn-up on the slightly downhill four-kilometre run-in.

THE ROUTE

Heading south from the village on the Tissington Trail, the running is fast, flat and a perfect warm-up. Leaving the trail after a couple of kilometres, you cross fields and run steeply downhill on the road into the village of Thorpe. After a short climb out of the village you leave the tarmac, climbing briefly and then hurtling down a grassy descent into Dove Dale. Following the path on the right hand side of the river – the route mostly sticks to water level but there are a couple of steep undulations to test your legs. Reaching Milldale, you're on the road again for a stretch but, thankfully, just as it narrows dangerously for the climb out of the dale there's a path that runs parallel to it. Watch your ankles and footing though as it's a typically jagged limestone affair. The final steep haul is back on the road, before crossing the A515, re-joining the Tissington Trail and either having a gentle cool-down trot or, as is usually the case with our group, a drag race back to Tissington.

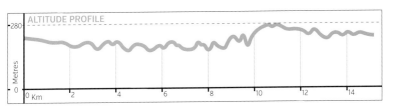

>> **TISSINGTON TRAIL & DOVE DALE**

DISTANCE 15.6KM >> *ASCENT* 293M >> *MAX ALTITUDE* 280M >> *TYPICAL TIME* 1:10–2 HRS
>> *TERRAIN* MOSTLY MADE TRAILS AND PASTURE BUT SOME SLIPPERY AND ROCKY SECTIONS
>> *NAVIGATION* EASY >> *START/FINISH* TISSINGTON TRAIL CAR PARK, TISSINGTON
>> *GRID REF* SK 177521 >> *SATNAV* DE6 1RA >> *OS MAP* EXPLORER OL24 THE PEAK DISTRICT
– WHITE PEAK AREA >> *REFRESHMENTS* HERBERT'S FINE ENGLISH TEAROOMS TEL: 01335 350 501

S   Not forgetting to pay and display, leave the car park and follow the signs pointing in the direction of Thorpe and Ashbourne. After just under 2.5km, leave the Tissington Trail, taking the footpath off to the **right** signposted *Thorpe*.

2   Cross the field bearing **slightly right** before going through another small field and emerging on to a road. Take the road directly opposite and drop into Thorpe. **Turn left** and **then right** and, after about 200m, you'll come to a car park with a toilet and a signpost for the path into Dove Dale. Follow the path past the quarry and then drop down to the **left**.

3   Once in Dove Dale follow the clear and well maintained path on the **right hand side** of the river. It occasionally climbs up away from the river, including a nasty long run of steps, but it's obvious to follow and always returns you back to river level.

4   Once you get to Milldale, cross the small bridge and then take the road that hugs the river. Stay on this road for about 300m as it bears round to the **right** and crosses a bridge. Take the path off to the **right** that follows the road. The path re-joins the road, keep heading upwards and then take a **left fork** for a final steep slog. After the road levels out, **take care** crossing the A515 and re-join the Tissington Trail. **Turn right** on to the trail and follow it for just over 4km back to Tissington.

FORGET THE CROWDS OF THE LONDON MARATHON, COMPETING IN THE EDALE SKYLINE RACE CAN BE LONELY!

21.3km

INTRODUCTION

This run lulls you into a false sense of security and gives a high average speed in the first six kilometres, with easy running on road, footpath and made trails. It then hits you with a brutal climb, rocky trails and the peat bogs that Bleaklow is infamous for. It's an amazingly wild and atmospheric place and the fast and technical descent down Doctor's Gate lets you open your legs and gain back some time.

THE ROUTE

Climbing out of Glossop on the road gives you a good chance to get warmed up but, after a couple of kilometres, you leave tarmac and run across fields to the Trans Pennine Trail. Make the most of the flat and easy running as you soon turn on to the Pennine Way and start the slog to Clough Edge. Even when the trail flattens, your rhythm is continually broken by rocks, streams and shoe-sucking bogs. It's challenging running but a lot of fun! Eventually you reach the run's high point at Bleaklow Head, not the most spectacular summit but moodily magnificent. Check your compass bearing and begin the long descent to the finish. Watch out on the slabbed sections as they can be slippery and are interspersed by some top notch high speed bog and rock hopping. Before reaching the A57 Snake Pass road, you turn on to the ancient Roman Road, Doctor's Gate. Not the pinnacle of Roman building, but fast technical running through an impressive valley that spits you out in the heart of Glossop – where we'd highly recommend treating yourself to a traditional Wimberry Pie from the award-winning J. W. Mettrick & Son on the high street.

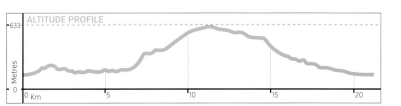

ALTITUDE PROFILE

633

Metres

0 Km 5 10 15 20

›› **BLEAKLOW BASH**

DISTANCE 21.3KM ›› *ASCENT* 696M ›› *MAX ALTITUDE* 633M ›› *TYPICAL TIME* 2:30–4 HRS ›› *TERRAIN* A BIT OF EVERYTHING FROM ROAD TO RUNNER-SWALLOWING BOGS ›› *NAVIGATION* IT'S VERY EASY TO GET DISORIENTED ON BLEAKLOW SO A MAP AND COMPASS ARE STRONGLY RECOMMENDED ›› *START/FINISH* GLOSSOP TOWN CENTRE ›› *GRID REF* SK 034940 ›› *SATNAV* SK13 8PN ›› *OS MAP* EXPLORER OL1 THE PEAK DISTRICT – DARK PEAK AREA ›› *REFRESHMENTS* LOTS IN GLOSSOP

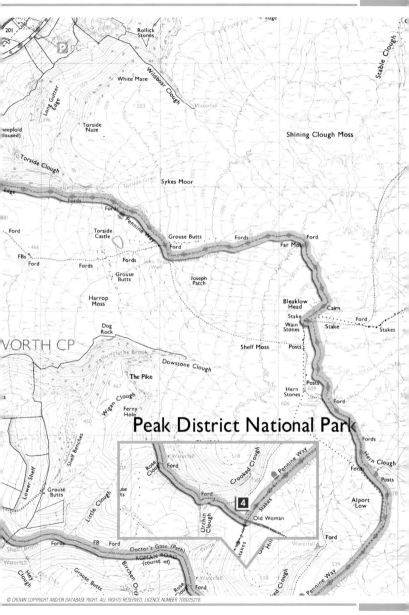

Peak District National Park

DIRECTIONS >> BLEAKLOW BASH

S Leave the crossroads in Glossop town centre, heading uphill and north up Norfolk Street/B6105 and past the station. After just over 1km, **turn left** on to Cemetery Road and then, after a further 400m, **turn right** into the cemetery. Run for about 100m keeping a keen eye out for the slightly obscured footpath off to the **left**. Take this path and enjoy the descent through the fields. Cross the road and pick up the footpath opposite you and, after a series of stiles, emerge on the road through Padfield.

2 **Turn left** on the road and, after a short distance, take the footpath to your **right**. It's a bit hidden and the sign is obscured from this direction but if you come to the road off to your left, you've gone too far. Head downhill, across the fields and pick up the Trans Pennine Trail. Stay on the trail for about 2.5km before coming to the B6105. **Turn right** on to the Pennine Way.

3 Follow the obvious footpath up on to Clough Edge and then the well-worn Pennine Way to the summit cairn of Bleaklow Head. Leaving the summit can be tricky so **get out your compass** and head off on a **south-south-west direction**. You'll soon pick up the obvious track. Keep following this over paved sections and along stream channels in a generally southerly direction.

4 After just under 3.5km from the summit, **turn right** on to Doctor's Gate. Follow this clear path down the valley, crossing bogs and a footbridge. Eventually you'll join a wider track. Keep right at a T-junction and eventually emerge near factory premises – **keep straight ahead** and you'll come to a T-junction with a road in Old Glossop. **Turn left** and, after 600m, **turn right** on to the A57 which will take you back to the start and your Wimberry Pie.

ON THE KINDER PLATEAU

22 >> TOUR OF KINDER

approx. 28km

INTRODUCTION

A stiff climb and a punishing descent sandwich an anti-clockwise tour of the Kinder Plateau – a run full of contrasts. You'll experience shoe-sucking bogs one minute and gritstone boulders the next. Kinder Downfall on a summer weekend can be like Piccadilly Circus, while at the plateau's eastern end you often won't see another soul. Take the distance and ascent with a pinch of salt as, depending on how strictly you stick to the edge, you'll never run exactly the same route twice.

THE ROUTE

After a warm-up on the road to Edale, we've chosen the Ringing Roger route on to the plateau. It might be brutally steep but it gets the climb done quickly and is usually quieter than Jacob's Ladder or Grindsbrook Clough. Once up, your anti-clockwise circuit begins and, as the whole plateau tilts slightly, it starts on a gentle downhill. As you head east, you're likely to see fewer and fewer people and, at your most easterly point by the Madwoman's Stones, you'll rarely see a soul. Turning on to the northern edges the route gets even more remote. If you think you've bitten off too much, this stretch is your best bail out. Take a southerly bearing and tackle the hags and groughs of the plateau at its narrowest point. Otherwise, continue along the edge for some of the most spectacular and wild scenery Kinder has to offer. Rounding Ashop Head, you're on to the Pennine Way and passing Kinder Downfall – expect to see a lot more people. Once on the southern edge, passing Noe Stool and the Wool Packs, you're almost done, but save some strength – the steep descent of Ringing Roger is still to come.

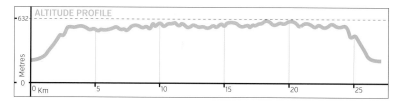

ALTITUDE PROFILE

632 — Metres — 0

0 Km   5   10   15   20   25

>> TOUR OF KINDER

DISTANCE APPROX. 28KM >> **ASCENT** APPROX. 700M >> **MAX ALTITUDE** 632M >> **TYPICAL TIME** 3-5+ HRS >> **TERRAIN** HIGH MOORLAND, PEAT BOGS, FLAGSTONES AND ROCKY PATHS >> **NAVIGATION** EASY ON A CLEAR DAY BUT DEVILISHLY TRICKY WHEN THE CLAG IS DOWN. REQUIRES SKILL WITH MAP AND COMPASS >> **START/FINISH** EDALE MAIN CAR PARK >> **GRID REF** SK 124853 >> **SATNAV** S33 7ZA >> **OS MAP** EXPLORER OL1 THE PEAK DISTRICT – DARK PEAK AREA >> **REFRESHMENTS** PENNY POT CAFE, EDALE TEL: 01433 670 293

DIRECTIONS >> TOUR OF KINDER

S Leave the car park via the steps beside the toilet block, **turn right** on to the road and head up towards Edale village, passing the Moorland Centre on your right. Head straight up past the Nag's Head pub and then take the footpath off to the **right**, down over a footbridge and then up some steps.

2 Start on the flagstones but, as they turn left to go up Grindsbrook Clough, **go straight up** the field to the gate and follow the zigzag path up to Ringing Roger.

3 At the top of the climb, **turn right** and make your way round the edge of the plateau. There are numerous trods and paths and how close you stick to the edge is up to you. You'll be running on soft peat, hopping from rock to rock and spending some time on flagstones. The route is relatively obvious – keep the drop off the plateau on your right and the centre of the plateau on your left and you'll be fine. The route certainly has some ups and downs but, if you find yourself descending for a significant period of time, you've gone wrong. Tick off significant landmarks as you go – you'll pass Ashop Head, Kinder Downfall, Red Brook, Kinder Low, Swine's Back, Noe Stool, the Wool Packs and Grindsbrook Clough.

4 After your circuit, retrace your steps back down Ringing Roger and back to the car park but maybe with a pint in the Nag's Head as a reward.

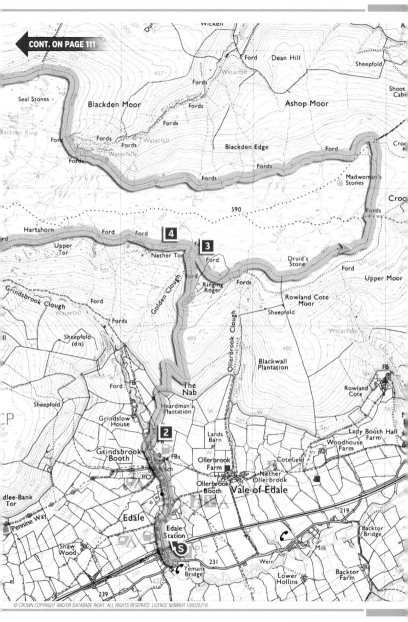

CONT. ON PAGE 111

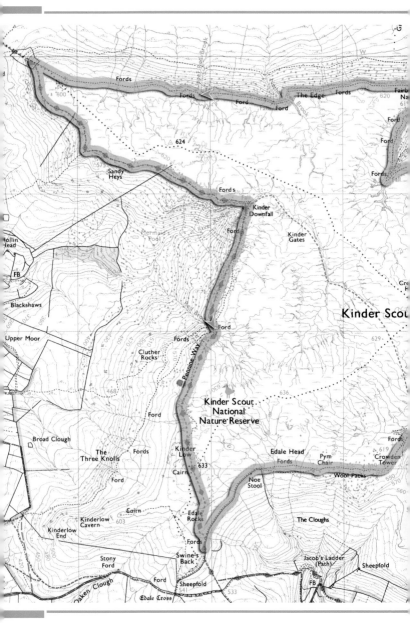

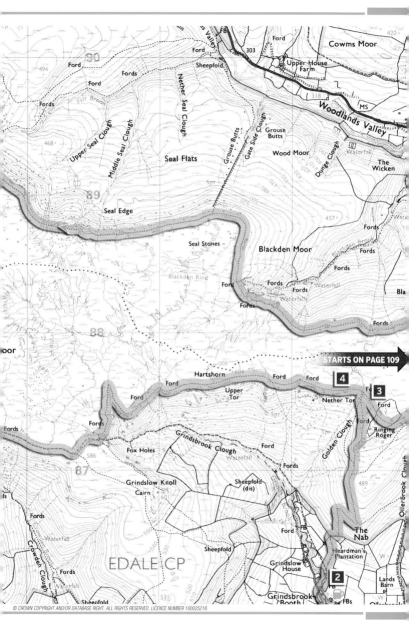

>> APPENDIX

The following is a list of Tourist Information Centres, shops, cafes, pubs, websites and other contacts that might come in handy.

TOURIST INFORMATION CENTRES
www.visitpeakdistrict.com – Official tourism website for the Peak District & Derbyshire.
www.peakdistrict.org – Official website of the Peak District National Park Authority.

Ashbourne	**T** 01335 343 666
Bakewell	**T** 01629 816 558
Buxton	**T** 01298 25 106
Castleton	**T** 01629 816 558
Edale	**T** 01433 670 207
Fairholmes, Upper Derwent Valley	**T** 01433 650 953
Glossop	**T** 01457 869 176
Matlock	**T** 01629 583 388

FOOD AND DRINK
CAFES
(See individual routes for recommendations.)

Charlie's, Baslow	**T** 01246 582 619
Three Roofs Cafe, Castleton	**T** 01433 620 533
Stables Teashop, Chatsworth and **Garden Centre Cafe** at Calton Lees.	
Penny Pot Cafe, Edale	**T** 01433 670 293
Coleman's Deli, Hathersage	**T** 01433 650 505
Pool Cafe, Hathersage	**T** 01433 651 159
Hassop Station Cafe, Hassop	**T** 01629 815 668
Woodbine Cafe, Hope	**T** 07778 113 882
Ilam Park Tea Room in the grounds of Ilam Hall, Ilam.	
Bank View Cafe, Langsett	**T** 01226 762 337
Longshaw Cafe, Longshaw	**T** 01433 637 904
Hobb's Cafe, Monsal Head	**T** 01629 640 346
Vanilla Kitchen, Tideswell	**T** 01298 871 519
The Old Coach House, Tissington	**T** 01335 350 501
Roaches Tea Rooms, Upper Hulme	**T** 01538 300 345

PUBS
(See individual routes for recommendations.)

Nag's Head, Edale	**T** 01433 670 291
The Grouse Inn, Froggatt	**T** 01433 630 423
Cat and Fiddle Inn	**T** 01298 78 366
Cheshire Cheese, Hope	**T** 01433 620 330
Ladybower Inn, Bamford	**T** 01433 651 241
Waggon & Horses, Langsett	**T** 01226 763 147
Anglers Rest, Miller's Dale	**T** 01298 871 323
The Monsal Head Hotel	**T** 01629 640 250
The Royal Hotel, Hayfield	**T** 01633 742 721
Norfolk Arms, Ringinglow	**T** 0114 230 2197
The Old Hall Inn, Whitehough	**T** 01663 750 529

ACCOMMODATION
YOUTH HOSTELS
YHA Youth Hostels can be found in the following places. For more information please visit *www.yha.org.uk*

Castleton	**T** 0845 371 9628
Edale	**T** 0845 371 9514
Hartington	**T** 0845 371 9740
Hathersage	**T** 0845 371 9021
Ravenstor	**T** 0845 371 9655
Youlgreave	**T** 0845 371 9151

BUNKHOUSES, B&BS AND HOTELS
www.peakdistrictonline.co.uk
For specific information, contact a Tourist Information Centre in the area in which you intend to stay.

CAMPING
(There are many more in the Peak District; search online or call a local Tourist Information Centre.)

North Lees, Hathersage	**T** 01433 650 838
Eric Byne, Baslow	**T** 01246 582 277

WEATHER
www.meto.gov.uk
www.metcheck.com

RUNNING & OUTDOOR SHOPS
Frontrunner, Sheffield
www.frontrunnersheffield.co.uk ... **T** 0114 266 9591

Accelerate, Sheffield
www.accelerateuk.com **T** 0114 242 2569

Up & Running, Sheffield
www.upandrunning.co.uk **T** 0114 278 0000

Running Bear, Alderley Edge
www.runningbear.co.uk **T** 01625 582 130

The Bike Factory, Whaley Bridge (sells running kit!)
www.ukbikefactory.com **T** 01663 735 020

Up & Running, Manchester
www.upandrunning.co.uk **T** 0161 832 8338

Runners Need, Didsbury, Manchester
www.runnersneed.com **T** 0161 448 4444

The Derby Runner, Derby
www.derbyrunner.com **T** 01332 280 048

GO Outdoors, Hathersage
www.gooutdoors.co.uk **T** 01433 659 870

Outside, Hathersage
www.outside.co.uk **T** 01433 651 936

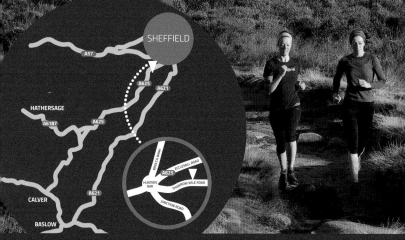

FOR THE
LOVE OF
RUNNING

Trail, fell and road running shoes, apparel and running accessories

FRONT RUNNER

296 Sharrow Vale Road, Sheffield, S11 8ZL   0114 266 9591
www.frontrunnersheffield.co.uk

Jo Royle Outdoor, Buxton
www.jo-royle.co.uk .... **T** 01298 25 824

Cotswold Outdoor – Bakewell
www.cotswoldoutdoor.com .... **T** 01629 812 231

OTHER PUBLICATIONS

Good Run Guide
Louise Piears & Andy Bickerstaff
Vertebrate Publishing
www.v-publishing.co.uk

**Day Walks In The Peak District:
20 Classic Circular Routes**
Norman Taylor and Barry Pope
Vertebrate Publishing
www.v-publishing.co.uk

Peak Summits: Eight Classic Walks
(Laminated Map)
Jon Barton, Vertebrate Publishing
www.v-publishing.co.uk

Peak District Mountain Biking – Dark Peak Trails
Jon Barton, Vertebrate Publishing
www.v-publishing.co.uk

White Peak Mountain Biking – The Pure Trails
Jon Barton, Vertebrate Publishing
www.v-publishing.co.uk

Peak District Climbing
John Coefield & Jon Barton, Vertebrate Publishing
www.v-publishing.co.uk

Peak District Bouldering
Rupert Davies, John Coefield, Jon Barton
Vertebrate Publishing
www.v-publishing.co.uk

**Cycling in the Peak District:
Off-Road Trails & Quiet Lanes**
Tom Fenton & Jon Barton, Vertebrate Publishing
www.v-publishing.co.uk

ABOUT THE AUTHORS

Nikalas Cook escaped London 'some' years ago and moved to Chinley in the heart of the High Peak. An experienced ultra runner with the Marathon des Sables, Himalayan 100 and Arctic 6633 under his belt, Nik and his two Finnish Lapphunds Moses and Otso have logged some impressive Peak District miles.

Jon Barton has been climbing, mountain biking, and trail running in the Peak District for many years. He is a regular competitor in the local summer evening fell races and no stranger to gruelling winter Sunday moorland runs to clear the excesses of a Saturday night. Jon is not to be confused with Nik, who is actually good at running, and indeed looks like he is too.

ABOUT THE PHOTOGRAPHER

Keith Sharples is passionate about photography and all things outdoor, especially if it involves the Peak District where he's lived and photographed outdoor action for years (and years). Shooting the images for this guide was a great excuse to re-visit some of his favourite places in the Peak and to visit some awesome venues that are a little further off the beaten track. Now that the pics are in the can (as they say) and he's not trogging round the high Dark Peak with a DSLR and a selection of lenses, Keith's enjoying going back to running some of the trails sans cameras and having a ball. See more of Keith's photography at *www.keithsharplesphotography.co.uk*

ABOUT VERTEBRATE PUBLISHING

Vertebrate Publishing is an independent publisher dedicated to producing the very best outdoor titles. We have critically acclaimed and award-winning titles covering a range of leisure activities, including running, mountain biking and cycling, and rock climbing and mountaineering. We are best known for our titles such as *Lake District Mountain Biking* and *Revelations* – the autobiography of British rock climber Jerry Moffatt, awarded the **Grand Prize** at the **Banff Mountain Book Festival**.

For more information about Vertebrate Publishing please visit our website: *www.v-publishing.co.uk* or email us: *info@v-publishing.co.uk*

ULTIMATE
DIRECTION®